BDSM
The Naked Truth
By
Dr. Charley Ferrer

Published by
The Institute of Pleasure
PO Box 60985
Staten Island, NY 10306

Second Edition -- Published 2014

First Edition – Published 2011

ISBN: 09770063-4-4
International ISBN: 978-09770063-4-2

eBook ISBN: 0-9770063-5-2
International eBook ISBN: 978-0-977063-5-9

Library of Congress Catalog Card Number Pending
Copyright Registration --TX0007553944

Editor: Rose C. Carole

Manufactured in the United States

BDSM The Naked Truth is similar to my book *BDSM for Writers;* however, there are several chapters for authors which have been omitted and this book has a chapter on Relationships all its own.

www.doctorcharley.com

For everyone who has ever sat in the darkness,
stared into the abyss and wondered,
"Am I normal?"

Table of Contents

A Note from the Author

Before I open the door and pull back the leather curtain to reveal the amazing world of BDSM—Dominance and submission, I first want to remove the veil of myths and misconceptions that obscure your view.

Through *BDSM The Naked Truth* you will discover the tremendous love and respect shared by individuals who embrace this lifestyle. You will better understand the emotional and psychological connections that are the foundation of a BDSM relationship and begin to comprehend the amazing dynamics associated with men and women in this lifestyle. I hope that, as you learn about the unique aspects of the personality types within Dominance and submission, you'll begin to understand how these unique relationships can burn so brightly, so quickly, and so intensely. More importantly, you'll discover for yourself that BDSM is neither merely a sexual alternative or sexual fetish that men and women outgrow with time, nor some type of pathological illness they're suffering from, but a healthy and positive way of life to be embraced and cherished—just like any other.

In order to accomplish my goals and provide you with a true representation of the BDSM community, as well as dispel the plethora of myths and misconceptions to enable you to peek behind the wizard's curtain, or in this case behind the Leather one, I cannot write this book from an impartial technical *how-to* perspective. As with all my other books on sexuality, I must speak honestly and with authority. And though I can do that in this book from a sexological perspective based on my extensive knowledge of sexuality, psychology and mental health, I can't provide you with the full flavor of the lifestyle without *outing myself* and allowing you to share a few personal experiences that I have observed or participated in over the years, which will help make this amazingly intimate, and for some, emotionally sacred path, more understandable for you.

So, regardless of *what side of the whip* you're on, whether you're new to the BDSM lifestyle, a full-fledged participant or have dabbled slightly now and then, you will find the information in *BDSM The Naked Truth* valuable and enlightening as it reveals a world many people misunderstand, fear and discriminate against, perhaps because of their own hidden and/or denied desires. I have no doubt *BDSM The Naked Truth* will become one of your definitive resource guidebooks when exploring the realm of Dominance and submission.

Use the *BDSM Checklist* I've created as a guide to unlocking your desires and your partner's. It will help you discover personality traits, desires and fears, and even become a resource to help you build scenes and erotic interactions. The *BDSM Checklist* will also provide you with food for thought on the various implements used to erotically heighten sensations and the various possibilities of combining positions with erotic toys to create different emotional and physical experiences.

Before we get into the heart of the book, I want to address two very important issues—disclaimers if you will.

First, *BDSM The Naked Truth* was not intended to be a beginner's guide on how to incorporate Dominance and submission into your life and your relationships, though it certainly provides vast information on how to do just that. Rather, it was my intention to provide you with an intimate look into the emotional and psychological connections men and women make with each other and with themselves.

BDSM *The Naked Truth* provides an excellent and unique introduction into the world of Dominance and submission for those who seek it, as well as validation—and dare I say possibly some new insights—for those who already embrace it.

For legal purposes, I'm always required to inform you that engaging in BDSM activities is both emotionally and physically risky and that some levels/extremes are dangerous and can result in serious injury and/or death. As with anything else that involves some risk, you should not only make the choice a ***conscious*** one that works for you, but you must also educate yourself by researching and joining the various BDSM organizations available throughout the United States and abroad.

Use the information in *BDSM The Naked Truth* as a starting point for discovery, I give you permission to research to your heart's content any aspect of sexuality that you wish and encourage you to return to share it with me and others so that we may all grow in our knowledge. Use the most powerful phrase in any language and let it open up a world of possibilities. Repeat it after me: **"I am doing research!"**

I hope the information provided in this book answers many of the questions you may have about this unique and erotic lifestyle. And if like me, you too sat in the darkness and stared into the abyss and wondered, "Am I normal?" please know that you are no longer alone. There's an entire community waiting with open arms to embrace you!

Now let's take an unbiased look at the world of Dominance and submission and strip away the Hollywood veneer of the Dominatrix cracking her whip at sniveling males who want nothing more than to lick her boots; pathetically submissive females who let men walk all over them; and the plethora of misconceptions perpetuated by novelists who have no knowledge of the complexities of this extremely erotic lifestyle so we can enjoy the adventurous allure behind the Leather, the whip, and the essence of love, sex, and romance that is the BDSM lifestyle.

Dr. Charley Ferrer

Chapter 1

BDSM in Our Daily Lives

It might amaze you to realize that BDSM is not all that uncommon among the general population. I daresay everyone has participated in some form of basic BDSM practices repeatedly throughout their lifetime, either during childhood, in their teens or within various relationships and family structures. The only difference is that the general population hasn't given their behavior a name.

It's imperative to remember that not everything derived from these activities is sexual in nature. Sometimes participating in them brings a sense of balance and comfort in an otherwise chaotic world. At times the individual doesn't even realize why his or her need is almost a compulsion or why it feels "normal" to do so.

What are these sadomasochistic practices?

Below are a few of the most common examples, both sexual/sensual and nonsexual in nature, which are steeped in BDSM dynamics.

Have you ever given your lover a hickey or received one from them? Why? Wasn't it to ensure that everyone knew that he *belonged to you*?

And what about those times that your partner told you, "If you do that again, you'll get a spanking!" Did you behave or did you purposely—blatantly—do it again, hoping he would carry out his threat, teasing him just a little bit more, calling his bluff?

What about those times when you begged him to thrust harder as he held you against the wall, driving you wild? Or was it you who pinned him to the bed or couch, riding him wildly until you reached your release, instructing him on how you wanted him to move and touch you?

Did you ever wrestle with your partners or with other kids when you were younger because you enjoyed the sense of power and control it gave you, if only for a few moments as you pinned him? Did you enjoy it when the boys blushed because they couldn't control their bodies' reactions? Just who pinned whom—and how?

Do you recall that boy who let you put makeup on him to become your living "doll"? Or the one who let you tie him up when you played Cowboys and Indians or Cops and Robbers?

These are all forms of Dominance and submission as well as sadomasochism. Let me break them down for you.

Those hickies you gave to your partner that you bragged about, proudly showing everyone that you "marked your territory," were signs of *ownership*. It let others know your partner was taken and not to touch him. And those hickies you received, which you proudly flaunted revealing the "treasure" kept hidden under your turtleneck or a scarf so your parents wouldn't ground you, were a sign of acceptance and affection, one that you promptly rubbed in the faces of those girls you didn't like or who had an interest in what you claimed for yourself. It told everyone you belonged to another. In lieu of a hickey, in the BDSM community you wear a collar around your neck. The only difference between a hickey and a collar is the conscious adult acceptance of that claiming: an acknowledgment that you belong to another or he belongs to you.

Those feelings of excitement at his threat of a spanking, which made you tighten your *tush* in anticipation and purposely repeat the behavior, was a desire to engage in the *power exchange* with another individual. To push against their control and have them correct you or show you their dominance. If you were providing the spanking, slapping his *tush*, was it the shock on his face that sent those tingles through you or was it the way he pushed you to give him more?

What about those times that you wrestled the boys (girls) to the ground? What did it do for you? Was it the power you held over them, pinning them to the floor, knowing that you could pit your strength against theirs and win—or even better, have them surrender? And when they became stronger, was it still exciting to have them wrestle with you, to feel the excitement in their body, to know you were the cause of it? Know that you could control all that strength with a look or a touch, eliciting their surrender…their submission? Or did you enjoy being pinned to the ground yourself? These were the beginnings of the *Power Exchange*. Not necessarily sexual in nature when you were younger, but instead a way to test your dominance or the dominance of another.

What about those rare boys who allowed you to paint their faces, put eye shadow and lipstick on them, who took comfort in letting you lead and following your wishes and at times your demands? That young boy who swore you to secrecy or struggled beneath you as you wrestled on the ground while you threatened to put lipstick on him and he didn't find the strength to merely push you off him despite his being able to? No, he wasn't necessarily gay or a transvestite, but perhaps an awakening submissive wanting to do things to please a friend—a young Dominant.

Then there were the boys and girls who loved to be tied up, whether to prove they were strong or merely because it felt good to be that vulnerable and trust that the other person would keep them safe. Then again, there were boys and girls who just loved to tie up someone else. Little Dominants and submissives in action!

We all start out somewhere. These behaviors were there in childhood even if they weren't widely acknowledged, shared or understood.

And when you beg your partner to thrust into you harder, needing his strength, needing to feel owned, to tap into that primal wildness, this is just another level, another plane, of your desires to engage in an exchange of power that feeds those desires and makes you want more, a power exchange that brings you closer to each other.

It is this same unconscious need for the power exchange that leads couples to fight, to engage in those senseless arguments that lead to incredible makeup sex. Because during makeup sex there's the unwritten rule that you can be as wild, uninhibited, and aggressive as you desire and your partner will not hold it against you. Ironically, it is this same aggressive, uninhibited behavior that is common and encouraged and is the underlying dynamic of the BDSM community.

As I hope you are beginning to realize, the *vanilla* (the non-BDSM community) and the BDSM worlds aren't very far apart from each other. We're just doing a lot of the same things; we just have different names for them.

Norm should never be confused with normal!

Always keep in mind that "norm" refers to a commonly accepted form of interaction or behavior, and "normal" is regulated and connected to pathology and, subconsciously, to judgment.

Just because BDSM practices are not the norm in our society, it doesn't necessarily dictate that its practitioners are abnormal or perverted. I remember when it wasn't the norm for women to wear pants in the 1960s and early 1970s. Yet that didn't mean the women who did were perverted or pathological. Now, no one even blinks when a woman wears shorts.

I'm sure you have your own examples of changing norms and perhaps your own curiosities about this unique lifestyle. As you read *BDSM The Naked Truth,* allow yourself to view the information and examples provided with an open heart and mind. Remember, just because you may not agree with the practice or certain aspects of it, doesn't mean it's wrong.

I wouldn't presume to tell you that everyone in the BDSM community practices or participates in these activities from a place of love, caring and respect; the truth is, there are those in this community (as in any other community) that do so from an angry and even pathological perspective. My hope is that you'll allow yourself to keep an open mind and nonjudgmental attitude as I share information.

Chapter 2

BDSM Fundamentals

BDSM is the acronym most commonly used to identify this community. It stands for Bondage, Discipline, Sadomasochism. BDSM incorporates various mental and physical aspects of interactions between individuals, both male and female, on various levels, including but not limited to emotional, psychological, physical, spiritual and sexual. Though this acronym and definition is the most common identifier of the BDSM community and encompasses all aspects, there are other identifiers as well, with different emotional and psychological connotations. Among these are Dominance and submission and being Master and slave.

It's important to realize that even within the community people engage in the lifestyle on many different levels and commit to one another in a variety of ways. What is acceptable for some is not for others. For the purpose of simplicity, I will use BDSM and Dominance and submission (D/s) interchangeably throughout this book. The aspects of Master/slave interactions will be addressed separately due to their unique nature and specific rules.

The term BDSM is used to define the entire community and includes Dominance and submission as well as Master/slave relationships, whatever the emotional or commitment level. BDSM is a place where some individuals who enter the community and want to merely *play* at Dominance and submission remain, never really moving into the more emotional and spiritual connections of this lifestyle.

BDSM also includes those individuals, both men and women, who merely want to dabble in their fetish for a little while, or just want some kink in their sex lives, but aren't interested in embracing the deeper emotional connections of the lifestyle. These individuals are in the community to literally roleplay at a fantasy before they return to the vanilla community. These individuals are not thought of highly within the community as they are seen as kids in a candy store grabbing as many treats as they can before running back to their vanilla life. The majority of individuals merely dabbling in the lifestyle remain at this entry level of emotional and physical interactions.

For those people who enter into the BDSM lifestyle because it speaks to their emotional and psychological needs, their interactions and play is more intense, often evolving into a romantic relationship that embraces the emotional connections of Dominance and submission. Depending on the individuals involved, the D/s dynamic can continue to become more intense, with a progressively greater level of control and surrender, and can ultimately evolve into a Master/slave relationship.

It's imperative to understand that BDSM is a distinct community with its own belief system and even its own psychological makeup. In a nutshell, it is not only a sexual alternative but an actual way of life. Unfortunately, as with any other sexual alternative lifestyle, it is mired in superstition and misconceptions as well as fear and contempt from those outside of it and, sadly, from within as well. Individuals participating in BDSM or accepting it as a way of life are often declared incompetent or seen as degenerates. Much like decades before when lesbians and gays were discriminated against because of their sexual identity, BDSM practitioners are discriminated against in the same manner, many losing their children, their jobs, even their family's support when they are discovered.

There is still a belief that sadomasochistic desires are based on psychological and pathological problems, and in some cases this is true. However, the majority of individuals who practice BDSM are not suffering from psychological problems nor are they axe murderers-in-training. They are merely men and women like you who have a different *love map* connection and express their sexual desires in more passionate, primal and creative ways. They are men and women who explore and even embrace all aspects of their sexual desires, including those darker needs that Sigmund Freud called *Thanatos* and that do not conform to or are accepted by the social norm.

Yes, there are individuals who commit acts of violence that incorporate sadistic practices like torture, humiliation, degradation, objectification, practices often embraced within the BDSM community. However, the major distinction between pathological behavior and normal eroticism is intent and consensuality.

As we discuss the psychology of BDSM, I hope you keep an open mind. Most people who engage in Dominant or submissive activities do not have a pathology. And though there is a misconception that individuals identifying as submissive or slaves have the need to be "abused" or to surrender their will to another because of past childhood traumas or an underdeveloped identity issue, this is not true. The truth is that these individuals wish to experience their lives in deep connection with another. To serve the needs of those they love and respect. To make their loved ones' lives happy and fulfilled. (Sounds like the same reasons people get married, doesn't it?)

I will allow you to research the psychological makeup and the numerous psychological theories of the pathology of true abuse on your own, as that is not the focus of this book. I will, however, address the essential truth needed for you to write your romance—what BDSM is NOT!

BDSM is not Domestic Violence!

In BDSM, when an individual calls out their safeword and says they've had enough, all interactions come to a halt. In domestic violence, there is no respect shown and the individual's request for the abuse to end is ignored. In BDSM there is never a desire to injure your partner nor be malicious! In domestic violence there is no regard for the partner being assaulted. These two vastly distinct behaviors should *never* be confused.

In BDSM there are safeguards established and honored by its participants to minimize injuries in some of the riskier activities. In fact, the majority of BDSM practitioners educate themselves on first-aid techniques. They also make sure to learn the proper use of the equipment they will use to stimulate erotic sensations in their partner to minimize and avoid injuries. An abuser, on the other hand, doesn't care what the end result of his violent outburst is.

BDSM is, at its core, all about power exchange. It is the physical and emotional manifestation of these interactions that lead to a mental or physical release, as well as the deep emotional bond possible with another human being. This power dynamic is what creates affection, acceptance and connection. It is through this exchange that the relationship flourishes and is solidified. Each member in the relationship is responsible for maintaining their role and interacting appropriately. Much the same as the traditional roles of husband and wife, the Dominance and submission (D/s) relationship is based on the foundation of these two roles to ensure its success.

There are very few rules in BDSM. This is a lifestyle where individuals make up the rules as they go and live within an honor system of their own making. This is no different from any other society. However, there are two fundamental rules that all respectful and honorable practitioners observe. These two rules are based on the observation of the safeword and the principle of SSC/RACK. A safeword is used when a participant in a BDSM activity is no longer comfortable with the activity and wants it stopped. Once the safeword is uttered, the interaction is stopped immediately. SSC stands for safe, sane and consensual. It requires that those who engage in BDSM do so with knowledge of what they are doing so no one gets harmed, and that all parties involved in the interaction agree to participate. No one is forced against their will. RACK stands for Risk Aware Consensual Kink and is usually practiced by longtime partners who may push the boundaries of SSC but who still are concerned with safety. We will discuss this further in the book and explain the distinctions.

Now that we've discussed the basic fundamentals of BDSM, let's address some definitions so you can better navigate this vastly erotic ocean of personalities and interactions.

Chapter 3

BDSM Definitions

In order to navigate the vast horizons and intricate depths of the BDSM lifestyle, you need to have a basic comprehension of its rules, roles, boundaries, and yes, even all those fun erotic toys and props/implements used and incorporated into the deliciously erotic, sensual interactions. Though I cannot cover every aspect of the lifestyle in this book, I will provide you with the important ones. I hope that as you grow in your understanding of Dominance and submission, you will be able to embrace the aspects that speak to you and develop a greater tolerance to those elements that don't.

Please keep in mind that these various roles can pertain to either a man or a woman, unless they are gender specific, such as in the Daddy or Mommy roles. And there are always exceptions, as in the case of switches and masochists, as these individuals incorporate more than one aspect of the following characteristics in their fundamental core makeup. You will notice that I tend to refer to men as the submissive in many of my examples. This is based on my own personal preferences and identification as a Dominant woman. I will try to vary the references to the roles. However, feel free to change the pronouns around to suit your particular tastes. Also, it's imperative to remember that the dynamics of Dominant/Master/Mistress and submissive/slave apply to both heterosexual couples as well as same-sex couples. Finally, not all interactions are based on sexual activities. In fact, some are service-based only, and there is no sexual and, at times, no physical contact. It's also not uncommon for a heterosexual Dominant to own a gay/lesbian slave/submissive.

Please bear with me for a few moments as I outline some of the more technical aspects of BDSM and share a few definitions with you. Remember, this is just an outline, a small taste, if you will, of the vast complexities inherent in this lifestyle. Use the examples provided in *BDSM The Naked Truth* as a reference point and build from there.

In order to simplify things as we continue, I will use the terms BDSM and Dominance and submission (D/s) interchangeably. I will also use submissive and slave interchangeably unless there is a specific difference between the two levels of interaction. I will do the same with the use of Master/Mistress and Dominant. It would help to understand that the Master/slave connection is a more structured relationship within the power exchange and BDSM communities. However, many similarities exist between Dominant/submissive relationships as well and both are just as binding. These relationships would be the vanilla equivalent of marriage.

So, let's get started with a few basic definitions. These are by no means the only terms to know; however, I believe the information below is some of the most important to include. You may notice that my writing style is very personal, so please overlook my jumping from third person to first person.

Vanilla
Vanilla is the term given to anyone who is not in the BDSM lifestyle. Everyone starts out as vanilla. Then your beans are crushed as you learn and explore and perhaps even embrace whatever amazing facets of emotional and erotic desires feel comfortable to you.

Power Exchange
The power exchange is at the heart of all the interactions shared in BDSM. This is the fundamental core of the relationship, whether from an emotional or physical perspective, which two individuals engage in—one giving, the other receiving. The power exchange can be physical, emotional, spiritual and sexual, or merely service-oriented. The actual levels of surrender and

control/dominance will vary depending on the individuals and what they desire to share with each other and to what degree.

Newbies

These are men and women new to the lifestyle. These individuals are often taken under the community's collective wing and encouraged to grow and explore, to do their own research, and explore their emotional and psychological connection with various aspects of BDSM. Nowhere else can your emotional connections vary as much as they do within the BDSM lifestyle. It may interest you to know that what you initially see as scary or distasteful and is placed on your list of "never-dos" when you first enter into the community may in time become your most favorite activity or a fetish you cannot do without.

Dungeon

A dungeon is where you conduct a *scene* and/or where you *play* with your partner. The dungeon is typically portrayed as a basement or concrete structure, yet in reality it can be anywhere you wish it to be. You can even designate a spare room in your home as your dungeon room.

Typically, you don't want to have your primary bedroom as your dungeon unless you live the lifestyle 24/7. Designating a separate room or area as your dungeon allows for the individuals, whenever they walk into that room, to fall into a particular psychological mindset. The psychological effects of that room will serve both the Dominant and the submissive. Unless you live the lifestyle 24/7, you want to be able to leave that environment to cherish down time to decompress and dabble into other aspects of your personality—and your partner's..

Designating a specific room as the dungeon allows you to have all your toys and accessories available and handy. Nothing stops the flow of a scene faster than having to leave the room to get something you've forgotten.

Dungeons are also found in BDSM clubs. Some establishments have various themes to their dungeon or various areas designated for specific play. For example: one area may be designated for medical play and another for spankings, complete with a spanking bench. Some areas will have pulleys or "O" rings on the walls or hanging from the ceiling so you can anchor your slave to these areas and whip them or tie them up and do other deliciously wicked things to them.

Dungeon Master
The Dungeon Master's primary function is that of enforcer of club rules. He or she walks about the dungeon, ensuring that the rules of the dungeon are strictly adhered to by all participants. The Dungeon Master doesn't typically interact with others, as his/her main role is to monitor all the situations and step in to assist or terminate a scene if he/she feels the Dominant is not experienced enough or has stepped over the limits, or if the submissive demands help or needs it. The Dungeon Master's word is final.

Scene
This is the name given to the actual interaction between the Dominant and the submissive. A scene may be elaborate and incorporate various protocols and/or rituals as well as assistance or participation from other parties. It can incorporate various erotic objects to elicit sensations, be sexual in nature or merely be emotional. Then again, a scene may be only based on service and not incorporate any sexual aspects. The scene is whatever the Dominant desires it to be, changing with his/her mood and/or the submissive's response. A scene can last anywhere from a few minutes to a few hours—even a few days.

Play
The activities shared by two individuals, whether Dominant or submissive, is often called play, regardless of the actual activity. Thus, play can be a flogging, whipping, using candle wax, etc. Play is often not really "play," but merely two individuals sharing BDSM activities and enjoying themselves. It can be carefree and nonrestrictive or it can be emotionally and physically intense, depending on the individuals involved. What actually occurs during play is called a scene.

Individuals will often schedule a play date if they are not living together just as vanilla couples plan dates. Play dates are lots of fun!

Service

When a submissive or slave is in service, they are performing a particular activity for the Dominant or their Master/Mistress. Service can be physical or sexual in nature. It can be anything from a foot massage to cleaning the Dominant's house, or it can be a function the slave/submissive performs, such as running errands. At times, a particular service has accompanying protocols and/or rituals associated with it. This is all determined beforehand by the Dominant.

Collar

Though collars have become popular accessories worn by teenagers and those into the Goth scene, as well as the vanilla public at large, BDSM collars are a sacred part of the Dominance and submission (D/s) and Master/slave (M/s) relationships. A collar signifies ownership and acceptance, just as a wedding ring does for married couples.

Nowadays, with everyone going out and purchasing their own collars, it's hard to determine who's a "free" submissive/slave and who's owned. Typically a locked collar means the submissive/slave is owned. You might see a lock on the back of a collar or you'll see a tag handing from the loop in the front of the collar, which might state, "Property of..."

The color of a collar may also have significance. The Old Guard BDSM community had many rules concerning the color of the collar and levels of service. For example, a light blue collar signifies the person is in-training and under consideration by someone. Therefore, that person is not available for interactions, and if you wish to interact with them, you must go through the Dominant/Master/Mistress who holds their leash—the individual the submissive is under consideration with. It is not acceptable in the community to touch anyone who is collared or under consideration/in-training without obtaining permission first.

Black collars used to signify the individual was free and available, but over time it has become the standard color of choice for the community, and both free and owned submissives/slaves use it. Gold and silver collars often imply ownership and a permanent relationship, although not all permanent Master/slave relationships are denoted by these colors. Some

Masters/Dominants/Mistresses will have a collar specially made. Personally, I created a Native American design for the collar I choose for my partner, with a matching one for me.

Though typically it is only the submissive who wears the collar, some female Dominants have used collars or chokers as fashion accessories. As I mentioned above, I wear a Native American necklace, which has at times been confused with a collar. Therefore, don't let the "collar" fool you. When in doubt, always ask.

<u>Limits</u>

Limits are the conditions and restrictions placed on behaviors or activities that a submissive is willing to conduct/perform during a Scene. There are soft and hard limits.

Soft limits are typically designated by the submissive when he or she isn't sure whether or not they would feel comfortable performing/participating in a specific activity. Typically, over time the submissive may come to embrace the activity or it needs to be tweaked slightly for it to be acceptable. Then, of course, the submissive may merely desire the soft limit to be taken out of his/her control or be forced to engage in the activity so he/she can override the guilt and/or shame associated with it. Soft limits can be broken. You'll often know it's a soft limit because the individual will state, "That's a limit…but if you want to…"

Newbies typically have a long list of soft limits since they are not sure how they'll feel about a particular activity. This is where the *BDSM Checklist* helps. It provides a reference point to start from. It provides ideas on activities to consider.

I often find that individuals merely need some encouragement and assurance that they will not be rejected after participating in activities that may be sexually extreme, outside their comfort zone, outside their designated gender norms or outside societal norms. (Notice I said *norm* not normal. Everything in BDSM is normal; it just may not be the *norm*.)

And of course, there are loopholes to soft limits. An example of a soft limit can be that the submissive states you cannot spank him with a hairbrush; however there was no limit against spanking him with a wooden spoon or a bare hand. Gotta love those loopholes! Or if the slave has a hard limit against spankings with a belt, the Dominant can spank the slave with a cane or even a flogger, thus, pushing the limit but not breaking it.

Hard limits are an absolute **No!** These are never acceptable to break. Hard limits are something everyone should honor. This goes for both the Dominants and submissives as well.

It should be noted that Dominants can also have limits of their own. These can be based on the same principles as the submissive/slave's limits. In addition, Dominants may impose limits on the behaviors and restrictions the submissive/slave needs to adhere to while in a relationship with them. For instance, the Master/Mistress may impose a requirement (a hard limit) that the submissive not interact with any other Dominants while owned by them. Should the submissive break this hard limit, he/she would be dismissed or severely punished or both.

That said, just because you should honor hard limits doesn't mean you can't push them a bit. For instance, if the submissive male has a hard limit about same-sex interactions, the Dominant can tease him about what it would feel like to watch him with another man. To push the "mind fuck" and psychological play further, while performing anal sex with him, the Dominant woman can call her strap-on by a male name.

Both soft and hard limits can be pushed to help the submissive/slave expand his or her ability to endure whatever is being done to them; to push them past a hurdle or emotional release or because it is felt by the Dominant that pushing the limit a bit without crossing over it is acceptable. However, whereas soft limits are negotiable and may be overcome with time and trust, hard limits should always be honored.

Safeword

It is common practice to give an individual a safeword. This is the word the submissive would call out when they need the scene to pause or come to a complete stop because they have reached their limit. It is the responsibility of the submissive/slave to call out their safeword when necessary. However, Dominants will often "call it" for the submissive or discontinue the scene if the Dominant senses that the submissive/slave is unable to continue, or the Dominant wishes to end the interaction with the submissive, for whatever reason.

The safeword is typically a simple word to remember, and one that is not normally used in a conversation. For instance, *Carousel, Unicorns, Pumpernickel* are all good safewords. It can be any word you'd like, although you will want to keep it short and simple and easy to remember.

The safeword cannot be "No" or "Stop"! When dabbling in situations where guilt and shame are intermingled with sexual desire, the submissive may feel the need to cry out, "No. Stop!" during a scene, despite their desire to continue. It is more often their sense of guilt and shame, or a programmed response behind the declaration, than any true desire to end their interaction. Also, their fear of being rejected or thought of poorly may also generate their need to call a halt to the activities. It is the Dominant's responsibility to ascertain which it is—communication is key.

When interacting with a Dominant for the first time, or if you're not able to remember or come up with a safeword, it's standard practice in the community to use the principles of the stoplight—Red, Yellow, Green. This helps guide the Dominant and gives some illusion of control to the submissive. Using Red, Yellow, and Green allows both participants to know the submissive's level of comfort and desire to continue playing.

Let me break it down for you:

• Green means "Everything is okay and wonderful, please continue."

• Yellow means the Dominant is pushing boundaries, and the submissive may need to slow down or talk but is willing to continue.

• Red calls a halt either to that particular activity or the whole scene.

For example, one slave was happily receiving a flogging, but when the Dominant began to tickle her, she screamed, "Red. Red. I hate tickling." The Dominant immediately ceased tickling, continued flogging her, and the rest of the scene continued.

SSC
SSC stands for Safe, Sane and Consensual. Within the community it is one of the fundamental rules of engagement.

Those who break this rule are thought to be dangerous, and many BDSMers will steer clear of them.

Despite the thousands, even millions, of BDSM practitioners in the world, the BDSM community as a whole is still small, and word travels quickly. It is not uncommon for individuals in Texas to know which specific individuals in New York City violated SSC. Also, with the popularity of the Internet and the fact that various groups hold events throughout the country and the world, it's easy for word to circulate. The BDSM community has an amazing grapevine.

RACK

RACK stands for Risk Aware Consensual Kink. Unlike those who practice SSC, individuals who embrace RACK engage in more intense BDSM interactions. The basic concept of consensual non-consensuality, an advanced form of BDSM edge play, is the fact that you willingly and consciously consent NOT to have any rights to object to what is done to you. Thus, you consent beforehand to interactions governed by another individual and whatever he or she deems desirous and/or appropriate. This is not something recommended or typically engaged in by newbies. Even some experienced practitioners do not enter into this realm. Individuals who participate in this level of interaction typically play at higher levels of intensity; both emotionally and physically. It is important to remember, this level of interaction is an individual choice.

Let's not forget it is the Dominant's prerogative to push the submissive further than he or she thought was possible, whether emotionally or physically. And though it may seem excessive or abusive to you, rest assured that the Dominant is keeping the needs and safety of the submissive uppermost in His/Her mind.

Etiquettes

Etiquettes are typically the common courtesies used in everyday life, with just a bit more formality. They tend to be individual preferences and can change as needed or desired. Each household has its own etiquettes though standard honorifics are commonplace. When speaking to a Mistress/Master the slave/submissive uses Ma'am or Sir or whatever title the Dominant desires.

Dominant women tend to require typical common chivalrous practices from their slaves, like opening the door for them, seeing to their needs in public, even ordering a meal at a restaurant for them, once the slave has been told what She wants of course.

Protocols/Rituals

Protocols are a specific way of showing respect. Protocols are specific dictates and behaviors each Dominant or Master establishes for His/Her submissive/slave. This can be anything from how the submissive stands, dresses or speaks when these protocols take place. There can be specific protocols for interacting in public as opposed to private settings, as well as rituals for how an individual is required to interact during vanilla events in comparison to D/s functions.

For instance, a male slave may be required to go naked with only their collar and cuffs while at home. He may be required to kneel before or stand alongside his Master/Mistress instead of sitting in a chair beside Him/Her. The submissive/slave may be required to obey eye-contact restrictions with his Master/Mistress, looking straight ahead or looking down when speaking to Him/Her. This is typical of military protocols, which many individuals in the BDSM community adhere to.

The beauty about a protocol is that you can tailor it to whatever you desire, and if you find that it's not working for you, you can dismiss it and implement another in its place or tweak a specific protocol to work out the kinks in it—no pun intended.

Protocol enforcement is the responsibility of the Dominant, and thus keeping them simple is best unless the Dominant is willing to micromanage. It's not surprising that a submissive/slave will sometimes intentionally perform a protocol incorrectly to attract his Master's attention and/or at times to test their Master/Mistress to gauge whether what he (the slave) does is important to their Master/Mistress.

Rituals are very rigid, specific and in some ways sacred. Ritual takes protocol to its ultimate form. Rituals allow slaves to show respect and reverence through the duties they perform for their Master/Mistress and for the interactions they engage in, from typical everyday practices such as how they present their Master/Mistress with coffee or present themselves for service (kneeling/standing in a specific manner) to how they prepare themselves physically for play and/or sexual interactions.

Dismissal

Dismissal is the term used for a BDSM breakup that ends the relationship, regardless of the reason behind it. When a slave/submissive is dismissed, his/her collar is removed.

Typically a Dominant will not reinstate a submissive who was dismissed from service in the past especially if their dismissal was based on hard limits imposed by the Dominant being broken. For example, if the submissive was not allowed to interact in physical or sexual play with another individual, but did (thereby breaking one of the hard limits—one of the major rules), they would not be welcome in the Dominants household.

Remember, the Dominant/submissive relationship is based on trust! Once trust is broken or a betrayal occurs, there is no foundation to work with, as the Dominant knows the submissive/slave is not trustworthy and would most likely be untrustworthy in the future. And yes, trust is required of the Dominant as well. Though the slave/submissive does not dismiss the Dominant, the slave may choose to sever their contract and their ties with the Dominant.

Dismissal can also occur if the Dominant feels the slave is not meeting the Dominant's needs or the slave/submissive was not compatible with them.

It is common practice for Dominants to request referrals from past Masters/Mistresses, or even fellow submissives, from a submissive/slave under consideration. Though ultimately it is the Dominant's decision whether or not to accept a slave, some Dominants will decide against accepting a slave based on the feedback provided. I find women more so than men will check on references and prior interactions and behavior patterns both from a submissive or Dominant perspective.

Negotiations

Negotiations are typically performed between two individuals who have recently met or are playing for the first time.

Negotiations determine what is allowed during a particular interaction and what is not. It should be noted that each scene/play employs its own negotiations and what was acceptable in a former scene together may not necessarily be acceptable in the current one. At any time during the negotiation process, one or both of the individuals may decide play would not be acceptable, often because the Dominant wants to be able to do more than the submissive is offering, or visa versa.

A Mistress/Master who already owns a submissive/slave does not negotiate the scene/play with His/Her submissive/slave as the submissive's hard limits have already been established and any interactions within those parameters is deemed acceptable. Often, once a submissive/slave is collared, his hard limits are those the Dominant has established for him and/or are the hard limits of the Dominant.

During negotiations, a safeword is established and an individual's soft and hard limits are reviewed and agreed upon. Both the Dominant and submissive must agree to respect these during play. Duration of lay is also established. For example, a time constraint can be in place: playing for two hours or half an hour. Agreement over what implements will be used: for example, deciding among floggers, crops and canes (or all of them). They also discuss techniques like knife play and bondage and how each activity will be performed. For instance, will the spanking be performed with a hand, a belt, or a paddle? Remember, BDSM is all about the psychological connections made by the individuals physically and emotionally as couple. We'll discuss this further in a later chapter.

Though negotiations are typically made before engaging in actual play, they can also be performed once play has begun. For example, an interaction can begin with a restriction on only open-handed spanking, but as the play continues the Dominant or submissive may wish to agree on the stronger sensation of a paddle or hairbrush. Or maybe it was negotiated that a whip would be used, but the submissive later requests to not have the Dominant continue using it.

Also it's important to realize that the individuals are constantly communicating throughout the interaction. For instance: the Dominant may be flogging the slave and occasionally—

purposely—flog between his legs, striking the penis and scrotum. The slave would then advise the Dominant that the force is too strong, as his recent vasectomy makes it hard for him to tolerate too much pressure in that area at this time. The Dominant then lightens Her strikes and/or moves to a different area of his body to torment.

Anything and everything can be negotiated, including sexual contact and specific sexual acts. For instance, oral sex might be permissible, but anal sex can be a limit. Or penetration can only be conducted with an adult sex toy and not with the other person's genitals. And of course, safe sex practices can be established and negotiated as well—something I always recommend if not in a closed relationship.

BDSM Checklist

There are several wonderful books on the market and online that outline various checklists you can use. I have created a specific *BDSM Checklist* in this book, which I believe will assist you in discovering your own erotic tastes and give you a few ideas on which activities you may wish to try and/or perform. You will also be able to identify which activities have specific emotional connections for you. This *BDSM Checklist* is a great guide and resource tool to help you develop and play with the various erotic activities, punishments, corrections and so on that you and/or your Dominant/submissive may wish to engage in.

Typically it is the submissive who completes the *BDSM Checklist* and gives it to the Dominant for review. However, I always recommend the Dominant completes His/Her own list to help determine where their own boundaries lie.

The *BDSM Checklist* is not a measurement of how kinky a person is. There is no judgment for being willing (or unwilling) to give or receive an activity. There is no good or bad. The *BDSM Checklist* merely helps an individual, especially the submissive, understand the vast possibilities in BDSM and, based on those answers, allows the Dominant to get a better grasp of where the submissive's needs, desires, even their fears lie.

For instance: spanking is a pretty simple activity. However it has many variations and each variation is wrapped in its own emotional connections. Let me give you an example: a spanking can be performed over the knee (commonly known as OTK), which carries with it some sense of humiliation. Now imagine the level of humiliation that would occur if the person had to pull their pants and underwear down to their ankles then lie across the Dominant's lap? Spanking also varies greatly if a hairbrush, belt or shoe is used instead of merely an open palm. Though it's all the same activity—a spanking—the actual emotional connections, whether conscious or unconscious, will greatly affect the interaction between the *giver* and the *receiver*, the Dominant and the submissive. (I provide a more in-depth psychological review on the benefits of the *BDSM Checklist* and the emotional intricacies it reveals in the chapter on the *BDSM Checklist.*)

It's imperative to remember that an individual's *BDSM Checklist*—those things he/she will and will not perform or adhere to—and even enjoys and finds erotic—is constantly changing. This is why I always have a slave/submissive complete a new *BDSM Checklist* every six months to a year.

Changes occur over time and are due to a variety of reasons. This may be because of comfort level the submissive/slave develops with whom they are interacting and as well as a desensitization of the negative emotions associated with a particular activity. The submissive may want to push themselves further or has worked through whatever issue it was that blocked acceptance of that aspect of themselves and/or their partner. It can even be as simple as being turned on by observing another individual participating in the activity. Perhaps he or she discovered when they tried something, they didn't like it or realized they weren't emotionally ready to dabble in that area. It's also imperative to understand and accept that what the individual (both Dominant or submissive) may have found extremely erotic when fantasizing can turn out to be distasteful in reality..

Edge Play

Edge Play is considered an advanced form of BDSM interaction that not all individuals in the lifestyle participate in. Though any aspect of BDSM involves physical and even emotional risks and/or consequences, edge play interactions are dangerous and can lead to serious injuries and/or emotional distress. In some rare cases, edge play can lead to unintentional death. I've listed a few examples of edge play below.

One of the more common forms of edge play is breath play, in which a person's natural ability to breathe is restricted by someone else. Asphyxiation is another form of breath play, which involves actual strangulation. This is one of the most extreme levels of edge play and is responsible for many accidental deaths; it is classified as autoerotic asphyxiation. This can be performed with a partner or alone.

Using fire as a conduit of erotic interaction is called fire play; this does not include candle wax. Fire play is considered dangerous because of the possibility of second- and third-degree burns.

Knife play uses a knife or straight razor to cut or simulate cutting on the body. A more extreme level of knife play incorporates actual penetration of the vaginal, penal and anal cavity. I do not endorse this activity due to its extreme level of risk; however as with anything else, this is a personal choice. I would strongly caution you against mentioning it in your novels, as it can evoke extreme emotional reactions from readers, unless, of course, that is your intention.

Fear play incorporates anything the person fears, whether physical or emotional, and can be used with or without actual physical interaction. Fear play doesn't necessarily have to incorporate an individual's actual known fears. It can be any play that produces the sensation of fear. Note I am talking about fear not terror. You don't want the submissive so fearful, they can't think or worse, go into shock. Also, physically speaking, keeping an individual on the edge of fear will allow for hours of wicked fun; pushing them into terror gives you about 15 to 30 minutes tops before their body and mind shuts down and they are incapacitated.

And finally, mind fucks are those deliciously sinful thrills that combine mental play with physical, pushing both the submissive/slave and Dominant to a higher emotional and mental level of interaction where reality is at times distorted and two contradictory truths coexist simultaneously, causing confusion and distress. The goal isn't to cause an emotional breakdown but to push the slave to the edge. *The Forked Tongue* by Flagg is a must-have book for people who want to learn some of the intricacies that make a great mind fuck possible

Humiliation Play

The complexities and levels of humiliation play vary from a simple tease to embarrassment to outright degradation. This is an individual preference for the couple. Not everyone agrees with or participates in humiliation lay. It's important to understand that humiliation play varies greatly and is vastly different for men than it is for women—not only from a physical perspective but an emotional and psychological one as well. What will trigger major reactions in a woman may be shrugged off by a man and vice-versa. We will discuss humiliation play from each perspective in greater detail in a later chapter.

Aftercare

No negotiation on BDSM is complete without discussing aftercare. Aftercare is as important to the BDSM community as foreplay is to the vanilla community. Aftercare is what happens once the scene is over. It is often agreed upon during negotiations. It is typically the Dominant's responsibility to provide aftercare for the submissive they have interacted with or to make prior arrangements for it to be provided by another submissive or Dominant.

Aftercare can consist of holding the submissive/slave and reassuring him/her that they are still desired and accepted despite their behavior during the scene. At times, depending on the intensity of the scene, the individual may feel a bit of embarrassment or shame or have an emotional cathartic breakthrough and need emotional support. Aftercare can be as simple as sitting with the slave for a while to ensure they are okay—especially if the submissive is just someone the Dominant is casually interacting with—or spending a few hours with them.

Oftentimes, a Dominant will contact the submissive the following day to check in with him or her and ensure the slave is doing all right or establish a check-in timeframe for the submissive to contact the Dominant conveying they are all right and in good mental health. Aftercare varies greatly between those individuals who are just playing or staring a new relationship and those who are in an established relationship. It may also vary depending on whether the submissive/slave is a man or a woman.

Typically, it is the submissive who receives the aftercare; however a Dominant at times is also in need of it as well, whether it's a back massage after a long flogging scene or reassurance after having pushed their submissive further than the Dominant felt comfortable doing. Aftercare for the Dominant is something that should be negotiated at the beginning of a scene if the individuals are not in a serious relationship.

Typically the Dominant is not provided service immediately after a scene unless He or She has more than one submissive. This is not because the submissive/slave is not willing to do so, but that in most cases the slave/submissive is physically or emotionally exhausted and/or are in what is called subspace.

Subspace

Subspace is an emotional and physical phenomenon that occurs in the submissive/slave during physical and/or sexual interactions. It can also occur during service to their Master/Mistress. It is an altered state of being; a comfort and sense of acceptance and well-being that occurs when the submissive/slave has reached a psychical or mental release and/or orgasmic state. It is a sense of fulfilling their ultimate goal and/or connecting with themselves and their Master/Mistress on a higher plane. It is where they let go of all of life and societal rules and requirements and achieve bliss.

Physically, subspace occurs when adrenaline and/or endorphins are running high in the slave/submissive's body and his level of cognition and/or coordination is compromised. Physically, the person becomes "loopy" and seems drunk or under the influence. The Dominant will want to watch for enlarged pupils and slow responses or incoherent ones, as these are all signs of subspace. In some instances the slave may even lose his ability to stand or sit and may even faint. This is when quick-release cuffs are a godsend. Having a chair nearby is always a good idea.

Because of these physical and biological effects, it's imperative to ensure that the submissive/slave is fully aware of his surroundings and is able to function as needed before allowing him or her to leave the Dominant's sight or be left unattended. The slave/submissive should never be allowed to go home, especially if he's driving, unless fully cognizant. If necessary, get a reputable car service to take him home. It can take a few minutes to a few hours before the slave fully recovers, depending on the emotional and physical impact of the scene.

There can be verbal, emotional, or physical triggers that send an individual into subspace. This can be anything from a word, a look, an instrument, even walking into a dungeon or private play room.

Sub-drop
Sub-drop occurs when the submissive/slave experiences an emotional crash based on their interactions and surrender. At times, there is guilt and shame from his/her surrender and the activities he/she engaged in or the emotional connection he/she formed. The slave/submissive may become extremely emotional, agitated or even teary during or after the interaction.

For instance, one submissive I knew began to cry as his Mistress was putting away their equipment after their scene. He clung to her waist as he knelt before her "thanking her for taking care of him" during and after their play. He stated it was the way she reassured him when he became scared and how she checked on his bonds that assured him she valued him and cared for him ,and that he had not felt that way in a long time.

It is not uncommon for a submissive to enjoy their BDSM interactions and a day or so later feel ashamed of those very desires and run away, refusing to speak to the Dominant or interact with Him/Her further. It is at these times that the submissive/slave needs the support of his/her peers and the reassurance of the Dominant, as the emotional and psychological upheaval can be devastating. The submissive may even undergo an emotional crisis based on who they believe themselves to be as compared with what they think their sexual desires imply they are. It can be terrifying.

It is this internal struggle that may lead a submissive to accuse the Dominant of wrongdoing, a situation in which male Dominants may find themselves in hot water—such as legal issues—and female Dominants may find themselves with a very aggressive and disrespectful male. Male submissives do not bring

38

their complaints to the police because of social stigmas; however, if they did, more Dominant women might find themselves needing legal representation and the services of NCSF (National Coalition for Sexual Freedom).

Also, it's imperative to remember and understand that we all have triggers from our pasts, traumatic experiences and secret baggage that we may not have worked through. These very issues may arise from a simple BDSM interaction such as a spanking or giving service (whether sexual or not. This is why most conscientious Dominants will check in with the submissive the next day or within a few days after their scene to ensure his/her mental well-being is okay.

However, ultimately, it is the submissive's responsibility to discuss these experiences—sub-drops—with the Dominant and/or individuals he/she engages with, especially if the drops are severe, as no good Dominant/Master/Mistress would ever want to emotionally injure another human being. In this situation, it may be in the submissive's best interest to forego BDSM interactions for a while and enter therapy to work on these emotionally devastating issues and become stronger.

Domspace/Topspace

As opposed to subspace, where the body is flooded with endorphins, Domspace happens when the Dominant is flooded with adrenaline and the Master/Mistress may be "floating" in their own euphoric sense of well-being and satisfaction. It is not uncommon for the Dominant to experience a type of mental orgasm due to His/Her interactions with the slave/submissive. However whereas the slave may become loopy, the Dominant becomes hyper and full of energy. Some male Dominants may even achieve a mental/emotional climax without ejaculation. And of course, a female Dominant may achieve an emotional and/or physical orgasm without sexual contact.

As with subspace, the feeling of total acceptance, completion and peace is also something the Dominant may experience, perhaps even a feeling of oneness with their slave/submissive.

Dom-drop

This is the term used for a Dominant who is experiencing a drop in His/Her emotions. Unlike Domspace/Topspace, where the individual is experiencing an adrenaline rush and feeling euphoric and hyperactive, during Dom-drop the Dominant can experience an emotional drop based on the interactions he or she engaged in with the submissive/slave. These feelings can include guilt, shame, fear, and even a moral questioning of themselves.

Remember, it is the Dominant who is orchestrating the scene, pushing the submissive/slave off the cliff; He or She is the one yielding the whip—literally. These activities at times can cause an individual to question his or her sanity and character. In essence, they may ask themselves how they could have willingly hurt another individual, regardless of whether that person enjoyed it or not. (Remember hurt not injured!) The Dominant may berate themselves for finding pleasure from engaging in such behavior—especially during fear play and edge play, activities that are extremely intense. The Dominant may even punish themselves verbally for finding sexual release from having forced their partners to perform a degrading act; or for causing pain and making their partner cry—especially a male partner. At times BDSM can make a Dominant question His/Her sanity, morals, even their very essence—and it doesn't help that society portrays those who engage in these types of activities as mentally ill, criminal or perverted in their desires. I find that Dominant women, more so than Dominant men, experience Dom-drop because of the standards and biases in our culture.

Here's an example of Dom-drop. A Dominant woman I knew had interacted with a new submissive who demanded she spank him, begging her until she finally relented. The next day, he accused her of "violating" him because not only did she spank him as he desired but she bit him as well. She was devastated, questioning herself and her behavior. It wasn't until another Dominant helped her put the submissive's behavior into perspective that she let go of the guilt she felt and realized it was the submissive's own feelings of shame and inadequacy that he was projecting onto her.

At times Dom-drop can occur if the Dominant feels they have crossed a line into questionable abusive behavior or the scene they participated in stirred up memories of past personal trauma. As with the submissive's sub-drop, working through these issues, discussing them with peers, or even addressing them with a kink-friendly therapist will help the individual overcome the emotional impact and allow them to move forward and accept themselves fully once more—or at the very least be able to place the undesired emotions into a more acceptable perspective.

Polyamory

Although not everyone in the BDSM community is into Polyamory, enough are for this topic to be addressed. Polyamory is a lifestyle in which there is more than one partner in any romantic and/or sexual relationship. In the BDSM community, polyamory is not always sexual in nature. It can be merely service-oriented or based on other physical, nonsexual interactions.

The majority, if not all, polyamorous groups are closed off to most outside individuals where sexual interactions are concerned; however, physical, nonsexual interactions with others are often permissible.

Polyamory has its own list of rules that are unique to each couple and/or group—each household has and makes its own. Enforcement of these rules is up to the ruling body and/or the Dominant in charge. Failure to abide by these rules can lead to dismissal of the individual from the group.

BDSM Household

BDSM Households can be comprised of one or more Dominant/Master/Mistress and several slaves/submissives. Each slave and/or submissive will have a particular role within the household structure. For instance, one slave may be used for sexual purposes, the other for household duties, and a third for professional or work-related duties. However, all the slaves/submissives will have one common duty—to see to the service and fulfillment of the Master's/Mistress' needs.

There are rules and protocols that each individual within the household adheres to. Failure to do so can be disciplined with training, correction or punishment, and in extreme cases, dismissal.

Each household is unique. Often Dominants/Masters/Mistresses will gather together or attend workshops specifically designed to address any issues that develop and learn how to make their households more efficient.

Munch

A munch is the equivalent of a potluck. Individuals gather together once a month (or more often if the group desires). During the munch the individuals will mingle, get to know each other or reacquaint themselves with friends they haven't seen since the last gathering. It provides an opportunity to talk and enjoy a little conversation and even negotiate with someone you'd like to play with. Most munches are conducted in a neutral setting, such as a diner or other public location, in which case participants arrive in vanilla attire and there is no BDSM play. After the munch, those who are going to play meet up at a designated home, play space or BDSM club. Some individuals open their private dungeons or homes to the group after a munch. I've even known a group that rents a hotel suite for the day and converts it into their own private dungeon.

Contracts

Contracts outline in detail the terms by which a submissive/slave agrees to interact within the relationship and the terms he or she will abide by. It may also include the protocols and rituals required by the Dominant. Some contracts are fairly simple, while others are elaborate. It is not uncommon for a Dominant/Master/Mistress to include a list of his or her responsibilities toward the slave/submissive and what they will provide to the slave/submissive in exchange for services rendered.

For example: the submissive/slave agrees not to date anyone else or interact sexually with another while under the contract; the submissive will make him/herself available twice a week on specific dates and times to meet with the Master/Mistress. The submissive will wear a certain type of uniform when in the Master's presence. The Master/Dominant in turn agrees to provide the submissive/slave with His/Her guidance and emotional support. The Master/Mistress agrees to take care of the submissive's sexual and physical/BDSM needs. The Dominant agrees to never abuse the submissive/slave in word or deed and to treat him/her with respect, all within the context of a BDSM relationship and for a specific length of time.

Some couples make up their own portion of the contract, aside from the basic terms, as a sort of "wedding vow" that outlines what they'd like to share with each other. It's very touching.

Most contracts are one year in duration, a sort of probationary period like an engagement prior to entering into a more permanent relationship.

Though the contract is not typically legal and would not withstand vanilla judgment and/or court enforcement, as no one can legally enslave themselves or another person, the contract is viewed as a binding commitment for individuals in the BDSM community. Those who do not honor their contracts are frowned upon regardless of the excuse given—unless, of course they feared for their safety. Remember I mentioned the community is actually very close-knit, and word gets around.

Contracts are sacred within the BDSM community equivalent to vanilla marriages, thus individuals do not enter into them lightly and are honor-bond to uphold them; however, some individuals do jump from collar to collar, Dominant to Dominant. Within the community, we call these Velcro collars, and they're seen as less significant submissives.

By virtue of the contract, the submissive technically becomes a slave, taking him/her from being independent and being able to set limits to being owned and having the limits imposed by the Master/Mistress as set forth in the contract. Therefore regardless of whether or not he/she is given that title to begin with or continues being called or thinking of themselves as a submissive, in essence he/she is now a slave.

****

I can continue providing you with definitions; however, that would take up at least another forty pages. For now, the definitions I've touched upon are the most important aspects and fundamentals of BDSM. As you continue to explore and research, navigating your way through the erotic and emotional complexities of this amazingly diverse topic and lifestyle, remember that everyone's opinion varies based on his/her experience level and perspective. What someone is comfortable doing today may have been an activity they were terrified to dabble in and share with another five years ago, or even six months ago. Thus, when conducting interviews with others for your research, ask the individual what it felt like when they were first learning about BDSM and what it is like for them now.

Never rely solely on the input of men and women whose only experiences are from online interactions, people who haven't experienced BDSM face-to-face with another, or those who've obtained all their experience from books or talking to friends. If they haven't actually experimented with and experienced BDSM for themselves, they can't really understand the vast complexities of this psychologically and emotionally rich lifestyle. (Neither can you, yet, if you're just starting out.) Nor could they possibly understand or have a true concept of the physical aspects of BDSM, though they can experience and share with you some of the emotional connections they've made. What they've experienced in their "virtual reality" fantasies is vastly different from the often indescribable physical and emotional connections formed in person. It doesn't matter how much research they have done, how many individuals they interviewed themselves, or how many books they've written—understanding the heart of BDSM and writing about it or discussing theory and your concept of it are two vastly different things. It's like being a male gynecologist— he may know the intricacies of a vagina, but he's never experienced a period, cramps and the accompanying mood swings.

Take, for instance, the true story of Tom, a male Dominant who had been interacting with Betty over the internet for over eight months before they agreed to meet in person at a local BDSM club. During that time, Tom and Betty played and interacted online four and five times a week. Assured of Betty's compliance and her desire to engage with him on a physical level, Tom tied her up in a public dungeon, caressed her, received her reassurance again and stepped back prepared to use a single-tail whip on her back; an activity they often engaged in virtually. On the first strike, Betty, the professed slave, screamed, "Stop. Stop. It didn't hurt like this online!"

Need I say more?

As you research and explore, it's essential to remember—even to train yourself—to reserve your judgment and view the various activities and behaviors of BDSM with an open mind. It's imperative to understand that what you might find objectionable and offensive is quite the opposite for another individual. It is easy to pass judgment on a person or activity in this unique lifestyle when you do not understand the intricacies and emotions associated with it or the complex emotional and psychological connections made. You may even find yourself clinging to those popular beliefs and prejudices that Hollywood and our culture perpetuate about individuals in the BDSM lifestyle. Doing so is no different than passing judgment on another's sexual orientation or religious beliefs. I dare say BDSM today is discriminated against as much as the GLBT (Gay/lesbian/bi-sexual/transgender) community was discriminated against twenty and thirty years ago.

Make no mistake, BDSM is not merely a sexual erotic pleasure or something naughty to enjoy when you're bored with vanilla sex. For some it is a way of life and an intricate part of who they are, even if they do at times struggle with their own self-acceptance. Please be respectful.

Chapter 4

Psychology and Misconceptions

There is a common misconception that individuals who participate in BDSM activities whether as Dominant or submissive have a few screws loose. All too often from a psychological perspective they are immediately diagnosed as having some sort of pathology and perhaps sociopathic tendencies. This is far from the truth! And yet, in some ways—in some individuals—perhaps there is a little truth to it, especially since the line between pathology and eroticism is so thinly veiled. In fact, in several states BDSM activities are considered unlawful even when performed by consenting adults and some couples have been arrested because of it.

Prior to 2012, the Diagnostic and Statistical Manual (DSM)—the psychologist's reference guide to psychological disorders—considered sadomasochistic desires and behaviors pathological and in need of treatment. (Just as they had deemed homosexual desires and activities a pathological disorder in need of treatment prior to the DSM-4.)

In the DSM-5 which debuted in 2012, BDSM was depathologized as was cross-dressing, fetishes, and trasvestic fetishes. The DSM-5 now considers these behaviors and desires "non-disordered paraphilias" and "atypical sexual desires not in need of treatment". That is so long as there is no undue emotional discomfort or distress to the individual, and the activity is consensual in nature.

I have to chuckle at that clause "emotional discomfort and undue stress" since many men and women who find themselves drawn to dominance and submission often struggle with their desires; especially submissive men and Dominant women who are in direct opposition to societal norms and the prejudices they've been taught.

We have the National Coalition for Sexual Freedom (NCSF) to thank for their efforts in this regard and working to safeguard our sexual freedom as well as the many professional and non-professional advocates who put themselves and their careers on the line to help bring about this change.

Legally, the acceptance of consensual sadomasochism is different in every state. In some states, even consensual BDSM is a crime. Thus, every person should learn what's true for their state as ignorance of the law is not an excuse, and it can get you thrown in jail.

Have you ever wondered what these types of people look like?

Well, let me tell you. They look just like the men and women you see walking down the street or sitting on the bus or train beside you every day. He or she is your neighbor, your co-worker; dare I say, even the person sitting next to you at church. They are men and women like you who have families and jobs, perhaps even children. They come from every economic and social background as well as religious, ethnic and sexual orientation. They have the same hopes and dreams you have of someday having a home, a loved one and basically having a happy fulfilling life.

They might even be you!

I want to point out that an individual doesn't just wake up one morning with these desires. These desires have been with him or her since childhood. As John Money asserts, Dominance and submission is their Love Map.

These mentally healthy men and women do not participate in BDSM activities because they wish to be abused nor do they desire to perpetuate malicious acts on another human being for a sexual thrill. Nor do they desire to hurt or injure someone who's put their faith, trust and even their very life in their hands. They participate in these activities because it is what they've learned and find comfort and sexual satisfaction in. It is their Love Map, and yes, they are normal!

Hollywood and authors who do not understand the dynamics of this intensely erotic and diverse lifestyle have perverted (no pun intended) the fundamental truths of the BDSM lifestyle out of ignorance or for their own gains, perpetuating misconceptions and myths that have led to discrimination and bigotry toward participants; much as in decades past the same was perpetuated against gays and lesbians. And just as with the GLBT community, many BDSM lifestylers who are discriminated against have been fired from their jobs, become ostracized from their families and some have even lost custody of their children.

Yes, there are criminals in our society who dominate their victims and do horrible sadistic things. Yes, there are individuals in relationships who manipulate their partners and abuse them. However, these abusive behaviors are not the foundation of *Dominance and submission*. Though these negative behaviors can be found in the BDSM community, they are more prevalent in the vanilla community.

It may surprise you to learn that the majority of the men and women who participate in BDSM activities and embrace Dominance and submission as well as Master/slave relationships are honorable people who communicate their boundaries and learn how to engage in healthy relationships through various workshops and interactions. Unfortunately as with any other community, we tend to notice the bad apples first and this taints the way for the rest: Though I would love to paint a wonderful picture of honorable men and women and portray individuals who just want to be free to love and express their inner libertarianism, the truth is there are individuals—both men and women—who enter the BDSM community for the wrong reasons. Some use it as a way to exorcize their childhood and adult demons; to feel powerful because in their vanilla life they don't; and sadly, to be "abused" because they're so broken from their past life experiences that they try to find a way to recreate those past traumatic experiences. Regrettably, instead of going to therapy where they belong and can begin the healing process, these individuals turn to BDSM. The reasons vary greatly from individual to individual.

As for those who use BDSM as a spiritual or self-actualization path, they too find their own delicate balance within service and the vast array of power exchange activities.

It's paramount to understand that BDSM is not merely about sexual conquests or interactions. It is about so much more! Some relationships do not incorporate sexual activities at all and merely focus on various aspects of service or Dominance and submission. At times the relationships involve a spiritual connection, at others an emotional or physical one. Sometimes the connection is in the form of mentorship and acceptance, not only from the Dominant but from the slave as well. These roles are forever intertwining, blurring and readjusting as each individual receives what they need from the relationship and grows in a positive way from it—if it is a healthy relationship.

"When the purpose of the interaction is not just orgasm but another kind of release as well, one moves to a deeper level of relationship that is more sophisticated and requires more thought and communication."

A slave boy I know shared with me the passage above, which I believe puts into perspective the essence of BDSM.

Before I talk about the "frogs in the pond"—those individuals who enter the community for all the wrong reasons—I'd like to introduce you to the primary types of mentalities that comprise the community. These unique individuals who carry themselves with dignity and honor and respect the rights of those around them and those they interact with.

Dominant

He or She desires to establish a connection with an individual who is willing to give and share of themselves completely. The Dominant seeks someone who is willing to follow directions and be guided even when the submissive/slave doesn't always concur with the decisions made. The Dominant seeks a man or woman who will be there to share their essence and embrace the life the Dominant is trying to build. At their core, the Dominants crave to share the true essence of themselves, their desires and their eroticism with someone who will cherish these gifts and offer their surrender in return. As with any other relationship, the Dominant may desire to merely brush along the surface and delve into basic levels of BDSM going no further.

The Dominant is the giver. This individual is in charge of the relationship. He or She sets the rules, safeguards their partner, administers training and correction as She/He deems appropriate and desirous in their personal relationship. The Dominant also dictates and administers punishment for any violations of the rules and/or transgressions the submissive may be guilty of. He or She is entrusted with the emotional and physical safety of the individual He/She interacts with. The Dominant is responsible for establishing and reinforcing the protocols of the relationship. Dominants have an alpha personality and are used to being in charge. However, you don't need to be in a management position at work to qualify as a Dominant.

Ironically, most dominant males at work are actually submissive at their cores and more service-oriented women—at work—are dominant at their cores. I think this dichotomy shows the irony of our societal norms.

A female Dominant is often called Mistress unless she chooses another title for herself such as Ma'am, Lady So-and-so, Owner, Master, Goddess, etc. Some Dominants merely use their first names. It is a personal choice. When interacting with his or her Dominant, the slave/submissive will use Ma'am or Sir as honorifics.

There is a small percentage of women who use the title Master instead of Mistress. Personally, I do not like the name Mistress, as there is a negative connotation to the word. For some men, there is the expectation that sexual favors are owed to them or that the female Dominant has less value than the male Dominant. There is also the subconscious belief by some men and women entering the BDSM community that a Dominant woman is nothing more than a pseudo-professional Dominatrix and should be considered little more than a prostitute as "She is there to serve the submissive"—in essence giving him a "free" BDSM session.

Most romance novels, if not practically all, designate the woman as Mistress or have her slave call her by her given name such as Mistress Stephanie. It's your choice what you wish to have Her called and by whom.

Proper etiquette dictates that the Dominant is always shown respect, even in written form, by capitalizing their title (Master/Mistress) and their pronouns. For example: using a capital "M" for Master/Mistress anywhere it appears in the sentence and capitalizing any pronouns which relate to the Dominant such as the "Y" in You when the submissive is referring to them, such as, "The chores You requested were performed, Mistress."

The abbreviated version of Dominant is Dom for men and Domme for women.

Master/Mistress:

Though they embody the characteristics of the Dominant, this individual will take the relationship one step further into an emotionally and physically intense level of connection, which is not merely about playing and satisfying desires. This individual, whether man or woman, will explore the full spectrum of possibilities, opening the door to growth not only for the submissive/slave but for themselves as well. The Master has a willingness to teach, share and experience *Eros* and *Thanatos* (the dark shadow of desire) with another and balance the two halves of their soul. The Master's intention is not to harm but to enlighten; to accept another's vulnerabilities and teach the submissive/slave the power he/she holds within, since a slave who has poor self-esteem doesn't serve the Master nor themselves to their full potential.

Imagine a relationship based on trust and acceptance that is continuously affirmed; this is what the Master/Mistress strives to achieve. The level of control and commitment required from their partner is the key in these relationships. Masters tend to be more disciplined and structured than Dominants. There is a higher level of intensity and mastery associated with these relationships. Also, there are standard and individualized protocols and etiquettes that dictate the interactions of a Master and His/Her slave.

It is more common for a Master to have several slaves dedicated to various tasks in the Master's home or life than it is for a Dominant to have. Also a Dominant/submissive relationship tends to be more couples only; however there are many polyamorous households that practice Dominance/submission principles.

There are also separate community and educational functions specifically geared toward the dynamics of Master/slave relationships, which are focused on the development of the Master and of the slave, as opposed to the typical BDSM events and community play parties. There is also a belief within the community that as you grow in maturity and desire for higher levels of interactions with your submissive, you move from the introduction of BDSM and mere play phase into a Dominant/submissive relationship, and ultimately to a Master/slave relationships. Not all D/s relationships move into the more restrictive aspects of Master/slave dynamic even after years of cohesive and positive loving interactions; however, if they do, they still may not consider themselves in a Master/slave relationship. The beauty of BDSM is its ambiguous definition, thus leaving it to the specific individual couple to create and define the relationship that works best for them.

Mommy/Daddy Dominants

Another specific type of Dominant role is the Daddy and Mommy. Note that though they may refer to their submissives as "little boys and girls," their partners *are in fact adults*.

Daddy and Mommy Dominants bring their own unique behaviors and psychological connections to the BDSM table. Though they may be Sadistic and sexual with their *little girls* and *boys* depending on the role laying age, their approach to dominance is often based on guidance and mentorship. Daddy and Mommy Dominants can be more affectionate or more strict depending on the behavior of the "child."

Please remember that when I mentioned *little girls* and *boys,* I am specifically referring to those men and women who are of **legal age** and enjoy roleplaying NOT chronological minors. These adult age-playing individuals open their imaginations and hearts and fulfill that essence of themselves that they didn't get to interact with during their childhood or that they just want to share and explore more of with someone they trust to guide them and keep them safe.

Sadist

Unlike Dominants and Masters, Sadists are not necessarily interested in the D/s dynamics of the relationship and may have a more egalitarian interaction and relationship with their slaves or submissives. Then again, they may be even stricter in their rules, protocols and requirements. Regardless, the Sadist is nonetheless in charge of the relationship and the Master of it!

A major psychological difference between a Sadist and a Dominant is the fact that Sadists are turned on by inflicting physical pain and mental stressors, much more so than a Dominant and thus taking interactions to a higher emotional and physical level of torment. And though most Dominants enjoy inflicting some levels of pain on their submissives or slaves, whether through use of a flogger, a spanking, a whip or hundreds of various toys, Sadists create an painful and/or psychological intensity that would make your typical Dominant cautious. It is the sadism itself that creates a sense of *rightness* and *peace* within the Sadist's mind and body. The Sadist enjoys pushing limits and taking the submissive/slave on a journey of physical, emotional, psychological and/or sexual exploration. They will often engage in more advanced levels of emotional and physical interactions, such as edge play. Where a typical Sadist will push against physical limits and endurances, an Emotional Sadist will push against the slave's fears and emotional issues, thriving on fear play and mind fucks, which are the basis of psychological play.

It should be clearly understood that the Sadist is *not* attempting to injure the submissive/slave in any way; He or She is merely interacting at a level others may fear to tread. Also the Sadist, at times, will push His/Her own limits when interacting with a slave at various levels and may be emotionally affected by the same. (Think advance statistical evasive Ranger training and/or Special Force psychological training for a somewhat vanilla comparison.)

The Sadist in these interactions is **NOT** interacting in a pathological manner! There is never an intention to **injure** the submissive, merely to share a part of themselves—what they may consider a sacred part of themselves.

Sadists are typically very discerning and selective in their choice of individuals with whom they will interact, and to what level. Sadists are extremely committed to the safety and well-being of those they interact with. Yes, there are some who aren't; however, there are idiots and dishonorable individuals in all walks of life. As I mentioned before, in these interactions, there is no pathological behavior as there is no malice intended!

I find Sadists to be more loving and attentive to their slaves, especially after an intense scene, ensuring the slave's physical and emotional wellbeing.

The best vanilla analogy I can use to help you distinguish between a Sadist and a Dominant is that Dominant sometimes needs a "reason" to discipline and punish His or Her submissive/slave; a Sadist merely needs a place. (Smiles, okay, maybe that was a bit cavalier, but you get the gist.)

submissive

The submissive desires to be of use to the Dominant, trusting his or her gift of submission will not be abused. He or she longs to share that part of themselves they've hidden from the rest of the world. Their need to be of service, to take care of another, to surrender themselves completely sexually, physically, emotionally, to make their Master's/Mistress' life easier as that brings the submissive joy and actually fortifies them and gives them the strength to battle life's challenges.

Though the submissive tends to have a beta personality, he or she can be very domineering in their own way and often chooses to surrender to only one other individual—their Master. This individual is the other half of the D/s relationship. He or she follows the rules and is of service to the Dominant. The submissive role is not always sexual in nature. The submissive may be merely providing service to the Dominant in some manner, for example: house cleaner, computer expert services, preparing meals, etc.

It is the submissive's duty to obey and adhere to the dictates of his/her Master/Mistress. The underlying premise is to be of service. As a submissive, he/she typically has more liberties than a slave. One of the major differences between a slave and a submissive is that the submissive may a free agent and can interact with whomever he or she chooses to until they become the property of another.

Though the submissive may not necessarily be used sexually, they may be used physically. There is a belief by some in the community that submissives are not as dedicated as slaves; however, that is an internal debate within the community and at times becomes a matter of personal dedication and semantics as well as level of surrender.

Another major distinction between a submissive and a slave is that a submissive has rights and the ability to object to certain activities or requirements and can negotiate some aspects within their relationship—setting limits.

The best vanilla analogy I can provide you with is the difference between a girlfriend and a wife. More is expected from one than the other and some rules can be broken and forgiven of a girlfriend (submissive); however, they would lead to divorce if conducted by the wife (slave), divorce being the equivalent of dismissal in a D/s relationship.

In written form it is common practice for a submissive to use a lower case "i" when referring to themselves as they consciously reinforce the decision to see themselves as belonging to another and taking a more submissive/subservient role. Also his/her name is never capitalized, such as, "Dear Master, i have completed all the tasks You asked of me. Respectfully, joshua."

Please note, this submissive subservient role does not imply less value, but merely a difference in the equality and roles within the relationship. Following the example previously given, a wife doesn't hold less value in a marriage than a husband, merely a different one.

Sub is the abbreviation of submissive.

Sexual submissive

Though not all submissives or slaves are used sexually, the sexual submissive's primary purpose is sexual use by his/her Mistress/Master. However, whereas a submissive will defer the leadership role to their Dominant or be subservient to his/her Master/Mistress in all areas of the relationship, this rule/dynamic is not true of the sexual submissive.

The sexual submissive is typically very dominant in his/her own right and often has an alpha personality in all other areas of his/her life and only relinquishes control in sexual matters.

Outside amorous interactions, this individual is very opinionated and focused on what they want in life, what they want to share with their partner, as well as the type of everyday egalitarian relationship structure they desire to engage in with their partner.

The sexual submissive may also have very intense masochistic tendencies. However, outside of the sexual arena, their submission is not really present or is minimal. The best example I can provide of this dynamic is the general who goes out and leads his men into battle, then gladly surrenders to his lover only to once again take control of his life after that particular interaction is over. He can allow his lover/partner to take the lead in the relationship; however theirs will be more of an egalitarian union than the typical D/s relationship.

slave

As these men and women make the transition from submissive to slave, they relinquish their ego and societal norms to surrender themselves unconditionally to their Master/Mistress, allowing the Dominant to take the lead and rebuild or redesign their lives in a more positive direction, knowing that surrendering completely to their vulnerability and handing it over to their Master/Mistress will bring with it affection and acceptance unlike in many vanilla interactions where such behavior would be seen as a weakness.

There is an old saying in the community that it takes more strength and courage to kneel than it does to stand—and the slave embraces this concept. It is through their complete surrender that they find the essence of themselves and can then share it with another and the world at large in a multitude of ways. It may surprise you to know that often very powerful men, like doctors, Wall Street executives, even Special Forces soldiers are among the most submissive and/or sexually submissive men there are.

Slaves can be either male or female. Their entire purpose is to "be of service" to his/her Master/Mistress and make his/her Dominant's life simpler and happier. The slave gives up many of his/her "rights" (by choice) to allow the Master/Mistress to dictate the slave's interactions and responsibilities within the relationship. Typically, slaves will have set protocols that they are required to maintain in public as well as in private. Transgressions are met with physical and/or emotional consequences.

The major difference between a slave and a submissive is the ability to deny a Master's dictates. Whereas a submissive may have some say and veto privileges within the relationship and/or activity being performed (in the form of limits), a slave does not. Also, when interacting in physical and/or sexual activities, the slave has no rights to deny what is done or required of him or her. The slave lives within the limits their Master/Mistress has established for them.

Within the relationship, the slave has consciously given his/her agreement to participate in current and future "consensual nonconsensual" activities and interactions with his/her Master and others designated by the Master/Mistress in either a physical or sexual nature, thus becoming a slave in the true sense of the word.

It should be understood that, though the slave is objectified at times, he/she is very well cared for and held in high esteem and deep affection, even loyalty, from the Master/Mistress. The Master takes his or her responsibility to the slave's physical and emotional well-being very seriously and will guard the slave against any harm.

The slave belongs to his or her Master/Mistress!

It should be understood that an individual may consider themselves a "slave" but have no Master/Mistress at the moment. The emotional and psychological makeup of a slave is vastly different from that of a submissive. We will address this psychological difference in a later chapter. However, the bottom line is that the fundamental psychological aspect of a slave is to give themselves without reservation because it is in their nature—their very core—to do so, to become enmeshed with their Master/Mistress completely, taking their relationship to a deeper more spiritual level.

The proper etiquette for a slave when addressing himself is in the third person. For example: "Master, is it acceptable for Your slave to prepare Your bath?" Or it can follow the submissive's format: "After i go to the grocery store, i will clean Your home."

Regrettably over the years I've noticed that many submissive women who seek a Dominant man within the vanilla community actually find an abuser instead. It's a shame that these women don't realize that it is the above description of the Master that they seek, and perhaps if society weren't so biased against sexual freedom, these women would know where to look. Unfortunately, women aren't the only ones who find an abuser when searching for a dominant partner; male submissives experience this as well.

Masochist

A masochist is an individual who enjoys the more physical aspects of BDSM. He or she will engage in more physically demanding interactions and edge play activities. Masochists enjoy riding the waves of pleasure that pain produces in their body. For them, the pain they experience at the hand of their Master/Mistress is an intensely emotional connection as well as a higher level of surrender. Most masochists will not use a safeword, as they will allow their Mistress/Master to choose for them when the experience will be over. This level of surrender reinforces their connection and is often their way of overcoming their fears of the activity or reaching a higher level of consciousness through the acceptance of pain. (This concept of achieving a spiritual connection with the self or another is evident in many of our religious beliefs and is a major component of Christianity; remember the common practice of priests reaching divinity through self-flagellation. Or the belief that to "suffer" is a way to reach God.)

A rare subgroup of men and women sometimes fall into the category of emotional masochist. These individuals thrive on emotional pain and fear. Not all masochists are able to explore this realm.

Though most masochists are submissives or slaves, it would be erroneous to classify them all as such. Some masochists have alpha personalities and are very dominant in their own rights, much like sexual submissives. Thus, these masochists enjoy pitting themselves against their own fears, using the Dominant as their catalyst for this purpose; others merely enjoy the endorphin rush they can experience through pain. There is also the ability, as mentioned before, of working through an emotion—guilt, shame, etc., and using pain as the cleanser. In this instance, the masochist is *using* the Dominant as a gateway to overcoming or achieving his goal.

A masochist is considered either a submissive or slave and is treated accordingly. In writing they often use the lower case "i".

Sadomasochist

Some Dominants have masochistic tendencies but not submissive ones. This is what's called a Sadomasochistic personality. This individual enjoys the edgier/darker aspects of physical and/or sexual interactions with his or her slave. Like a switch, they will enjoy giving and receiving pain. However, the major difference between these two personalities is that this Dominant would never surrender their will to their submissive or slave.

For example: the Sadomasochistic Dominant may enjoy giving **and receiving** pain, however he/she would never kneel before their slave nor beg. This Dominant would also never be in servitude to the submissive. These Sadomasochistic individuals may also enjoy allowing their submissive to feel empowered by engaging in rough sex and force; however, at the end of the day, it is the Dominant who will say how much the submissive is allowed to do and when this type of play is over. Plus, a deviously wicked Sadomasochist may even lovingly make His/Her submissive pay for his rough treatment of their Master/Mistress at a later date and time, thereby reinforcing the power dynamics and their control.

Property/ Objectification

This individual is regarded as lower in status than a slave or submissive and is thought of as the Master/Mistress' property. "It" has no rights to object to anything asked of it. It is often objectified and given a number (for example: 4663) rather than a name or nickname. Its vanilla name is not used when referring to him/her. It can be used sexually or physically in whatever manner the Dominant decrees. This individual has an internal desire to surrender all and have no opinions, options or responsibilities aside from those dictated by its Master. This individual is typically found in the most intense levels of BDSM interactions.

Objectification occurs when a submissive/slave is reduced to the sole dictates of his Master/Mistress. In this role, the slave has no rights. They are literally an object for the Dominant's use. He/she (the slave/submissive) is there solely for the purpose assigned, whether that is to serve as sexual stud/whore, to withstand the restraints of a particular role or to act as particular object (such as furniture or living art—think of the Roman slaves used for this purpose) or for whatever activity the Dominant dictates. Some individuals are objectified in sexual service, others by being designated as furniture, an animal or something else.

Others forms of objectification can be implemented through the clothing the individual is allowed/required to wear, which strips away his or her identity and provides the slave with another. This may include wearing a full facial hood or taking away his or her name—their identity—and giving them another (typically a number or a "derogatory" name such as *dog* or *whore*). The submissive/slave would then only be referred to as "it" and when referring to "itself" would do so in the third person.

Force can at times be used, as well as corporal punishment. Though this interaction may seem derogatory or demeaning, it should be understood that the individual being objectified did voluntarily surrender to begin with and provided his or her consent to the interaction. In essence, they are repeatedly providing their consent to such treatment every time they show up to interact with their Master/Mistress.

This objectification often provides the individual with a sense of well-being and feeling of belonging. Some slaves will objectify themselves in their desire to be of service and to surrender all sense of identity and control to their Master/Mistress. By doing this, they have achieved complete surrender, which is their ultimate goal, what turns them on and/or completes them.

It's essential to keep in mind that what you may judge to be immoral or distasteful, the parties interacting in it find it erotic and freeing. Also, this objectification is not in any way abusive or an example of domestic violence, as the individual was not coerced or forced into accepting this role in the relationship. For the slave/submissive it is what's right for them and is an integral part of who they are. As I mentioned previously, BDSM is *not* domestic violence. In a domestic violence situation, the individual would have never chosen to participate in these types of activities; and in BDSM the property/object consciously and willingly does so.

Before you pass judgment, it may surprise you to realize that this training and objectification is very similar to how the military trains its new recruits, turning them from civilians into soldiers who obey orders on command—regardless of what that order is.

Please note this is not a derogatory position. Property/objects are actually highly valued and guarded by their Masters, as they are so vulnerable and openly surrender all they are to their Master/Mistress. Such individuals are rare gifts and highly prized by their Owners. There are, of course, exceptions: those who belong to disreputable or severely sadistic owners can be sorely misused in many ways.

One of the things to keep uppermost in your mind when engaging in BDSM activities is that each individual is different. What feels good and erotic to you may not be perceived in the same manner to another. You are the ultimate judge of how you interact with others and what you desire in your relationships.

The object is referred to in written form as "it" (always in lowercase form) and will refer to him/her self in the third person. For example: "Master, *it* will go to the store and *it* will return with all Your required items."

Switch

This individual incorporates various aspects of both a Dominant and submissive personality. They enjoy both aspects of the power exchange, though their personality typically falls more onto one side of the power exchange spectrum than the other. Within the community, Switches aren't always seen in a positive light, as some believe them to be merely submissives wanting to dabble in domination, or merely someone who wants to casually play at the lifestyle. However, others believe that a Switch is able to experience both aspects of the lifestyle, though not as intensely as those who identify as one role or the other. For example, you can sympathize with a woman about what it's like to give birth, however, unless you experience it, you can't completely understand the emotional dynamics associated with it.

It's not uncommon for someone new to the lifestyle to identify as a Switch, as they are unsure where they feel most comfortable. Many Switches start out/are considered Service Tops as they are performing a service for another individual, and their relationship with or dominance over that individual ends when the scene is over. A Switch would never be considered a Master.

Some submissive men new to the BDSM lifestyle will identify as Switches, since they feel guilt or shame about being a submissive man. Submissive men often have to combat their own prejudices and those of their counterparts—Dominant men—who may look down upon them for their submission and not consider them "macho" enough. Also, it should be understood that some straight men will accept control and offer service to Dominant men, limiting their interactions to physical interactions but not sexual ones.

Switches can follow either the Dominant or submissive rules for capitalization—they get to choose which protocol to follow. I've often seen them use the lower case "i" when referring to themselves, thus, internally identifying as a submissive.

Swingers

These individuals and their lifestyle choice should not be confused with BDSM practitioners. Though some BDSM practitioners share their slaves/submissives sexually with designated individuals, this is not considered swinging. It is at the sole prerogative and discretion of the Master/Mistress to allow or require the submissive/slave's sexual interaction with another person, regardless of whether the submissive/slave desires the interaction.

Where the focus for the BDSM practitioners is on power exchange and the power dynamics of that particular sexual interaction, a swinger's primary interest is in sexual interaction, not in establishing a relationship outside their primary one. Swingers do not necessarily engage in BDSM activities, though some do, in addition to swinging. Also, once an interaction with the Dominant/submissive is concluded, there may not be others.

It is rare that you will see BDSM practitioners actively engaging in sadomasochistic practices within a swingers' event, as swingers do not typically like to associate with BDSMers. Some swingers' events even strictly prohibit BDSM activities.

Now let's talk about the "frogs"—the wannabes—as they're called within the community, who create frustration and discord. Unfortunately their numbers are so staggeringly high, they actually seem to have touched the lives of everyone in the community at one time or another. Just as with the vanilla community, frogs feel they're entitled to behave as poorly as they wish. Please note that each example below can be attributed to both men and women, though I've stated the behaviors under the gender that I've observed it was most prevalent in.

From the Dominant Perspective

In Men

These men have prior relationship issues and somewhat abusive personalities, as well as personal-abuse issues that they're dealing with. They feel women should cater to them and are very derogatory toward them (whether Dominant or submissive). Misogyny is their motto. They look down upon the submissives (both male and female) who offer their vulnerability and feel entitled to a level of trust they have not earned. These Frogs (as I call them) often push their agendas, making the submissive feel guilt or shame for not offering enough of themselves. These Frogs may secretly despise the submissive for their ability to surrender despite the Frog's own need to control them, which can spark emotional abuse in the guise of dominance. These men will attempt to control Dominant women, and when they can't or their advances are thwarted, they become petty or disrespectful. They can be very charismatic and lure the unsuspecting or new submissive to them only to blame the submissive for their own failures and shortcomings. These males are the wife abusers who enter the BDSM community in hopes of hiding their nature in the guise of dominance and sadomasochistic practices. Unfortunately, as mentioned before, many submissive women find these abusers and struggle with their desires to please and surrender, not seeing the warning signs in time.

Many married men play in the BDSM community figuring their wives will never learn of it because they don't allocate the same value to BDSM interactions or they do not interact with the slave/submissive sexually, thus they do not view their interactions as cheating.

In Women

Some women—female Frogs—enter the community wanting to take out their frustrations on men for prior wrongs they've endured. These abusive women tend to treat submissive men like garbage and often require financial favors or "presents" from them. These types of women degrade the essence of a Dominant woman and create a bad reputation for all, especially because any monetary requirement pushes the envelope of "financial prostitution." Don't misunderstand me, everyone loves getting gifts; however, there's a major difference between a man bringing you flowers and candy when coming to your home on the first few dates and one being required to pay you a set amount of money to prove his submission is sincere. Though some men desire financial dominance, in this case, the requirement is "forced" and stems from a negative and selfish desire.

In Both Men and Women

These Frogs—both men and women—may remain within the community standards of SSC (Safe, Sane, and Consensual), though they will push the envelope into sadistic practices as they ride the fine line of consensual non-consensuality. Though the majority of honorable Sadists in the community thrive on this line of consensual non-consensuality, the difference between a Frog and a sincere Sadist is that at the core of a healthy Sadist, there is no malice; whereas within these Frogs, their malicious intent simply has not yet revealed itself. These Frogs typically feel powerless in their vanilla lives and use BDSM to appease that feeling of helplessness and vulnerability that they have hidden at their core.

You will often hear these Frogs speak of D/s as a "role they play," often compartmentalizing their vanilla and BDSM activities and refusing to interact with other BDSM practitioners (even their own submissive) in the vanilla realm. These individuals are often married and troll the BDSM community in order to appease their unmet sexual desire.

These Frogs also tend to be extremely rigid with their rules and protocols and believe their way is the only correct way, despite more experienced individuals trying to enlighten them.

From the submissive Perspective

In Men
Some men, especially married ones and those in committed relationships, think BDSM is a wonderful way to get their kinky needs met and they figure they'll never be caught because their wife/partner/girlfriend would never wander into a dungeon. Plus they figure no one from the D/s community would out him because they'd have to out themselves.

Sexually, these males want to engage the Dominant in some kink, often because sex with their girlfriends or wives is boring. These Frogs figure that if they join a Dominant women's group or a kinky website, they'll find a woman, pretend they want a relationship and get a "free play session" from the Dominant woman, instead of finding and paying a professional Dominatrix for her services. These Frogs make it hard for the sincere submissive who is serious about interacting with a Dominant woman, because many Dominant women have become jaded and distrustful of his honest gift due to past experiences with Frogs.

In Women
As for submissive women who enter the community for the wrong reasons, they tend to use it as a therapy session, working out their problems with authority or with abuse and bad relationships. They hope they'll find a Dominant man or woman who'll protect them and make all the decisions for them, demanding they be allowed to relinquish all their responsibilities, thus, creating a situation in which the Dominant will take the fall when things go wrong.

These submissive women, who would be better off addressing their problems in therapy, become very demanding and clingy and require massive amounts of reassurance. They will immediately label anything and everything the Dominant does that they don't approve of as "abusive." These women create their own rules as they go along and blame everyone else for their own mistakes. They hop from one Dominant to another to another in search of the "perfect one" who will meet her needs and make all their dreams come true. Often these female frogs will be accused of Topping from the bottom as they attempt to control the actions of their Dominant. (Topping from the bottom is where the submissive tries to control and dictate the scene and what is done to them, instead of letting the Dominant retain control.)

In Both Men and Women

Another trait that immediately identifies these Frogs is their insistence that the Dominant set all the rules, thus taking no responsibility whatsoever for their submission or for the relationship itself. Whereas a slave or submissive will offer their will and their vulnerability to their Master/Mistress because they desire to serve at that intense level of connection and commitment, these Frogs merely want the ability to be as "bad" as they can get away with in a relationship then accuse the Dominant of not being able to "control" them.

There are even submissives who enter into a BDSM relationship or merely play with a Dominant taking more punishment or physical pain than they are able to because they crave the aftercare that will follow. These extremely damaged and abused individuals would do better in therapy but refuse to address their issues head-on. These damaged individuals will experience a 20-minute flogging scene and require an hour-plus of aftercare. They may even demand it in specific ways or deem the Dominant "abusive" if they didn't receive their "punishment" or their aftercare precisely the way they demanded. These individuals are very toxic for the Dominant as well as themselves!

***

The essential thing to remember about the BDSM lifestyle is that it is exactly like any other community around. It has its good apples and bad seeds. The only difference here is that coming across a bad seed can literally get you injured or killed. These are the reasons why the D/s community tends to police itself, since anything bad that happens reflects poorly on the rest of the community as a whole.

Chapter 5

Personality Traits

As we peek further behind the Leather curtain, it's my sincere hope that you will gain a more accurate understanding of the emotional and psychological characteristics of men and women, both Dominant and submissive, who embrace the BDSM lifestyle. Hopefully any misconceptions or fears you may have concerning Dominance and submission will begin to dissipate. And though I am by no means trying to recruit you into the BDSM lifestyle, perhaps by having an accurate understanding of it, you will be able to put aside any misconceptions or biases and have greater tolerance for yourself, someone you love, or even a stranger who identify with these particular traits.

Keep in mind that BDSM is all about degrees, and everyone interacts at different levels according to their comfort zone. I've used my own personal preference of the Dominant woman and male submissive dynamic for my examples; however these genders roles are interchangeable. Though I've provided some gender specific examples as well, I won't be able to provide them all; you will get the general idea.

The Dominant/Sadist Perspective

Unlike popular misconceptions perpetuated by bad BDSM movies and books, Dominants aren't the unfeeling emotionally distant bastards who greedily demand tremendous feats of submission only to neglect their submissive's efforts of service and toss a few gratuitous comments of appreciation here and there. Neither do they yell and scream at their submissives to get them motivated like the drill sergeants in the old war movies. If you stop to think about it, anyone who has to yell and scream is actually showing a lack of control!

In the D/s realm, lack of control indicates inability to take command of a situation and doesn't encourage a submissive's trust or confidence. Typically only an inexperienced submissive would accept such behavior from their Dominant unless yelling and screaming was actually part of a scene they were specifically engaged in or forms of play they created together.

A common misconception is the idea that a confident Dominant would circle around trying to pick up a submissive, jumping from one to the other at a gathering hoping someone would play with them. Yes, I have seen several men and women do this, however it is seen as pathetic by the community. One male Dominant I've seen always dragged his little bag of toys back and forth (on rollers) hoping to find someone to play with on any given club night. The really sad part about this was he looked so needy and pathetic, no one ever took him seriously. Some frog Dominants, typically males, will circle like a shark waiting for a newbie they can spank—someone who doesn't yet know any better.

Then there are the confident Dominants who carry on their conversations with friends, keeping an eye out for submissives of quality observing them from afar and nodding to them in acknowledgement, then letting the submissive come to them. This confident Dominant would complete their conversation, then either call the submissive to them or continue observing the submissive quietly, taking their measure and awaiting another day to approach them.

Another comical and common misconception is that every Dominant wants the submissive/slave to kneel before them before the submissive is allowed to speak to them. Personally, I hate when an unknown submissive kneels in front of me without permission. First, because if I didn't notice he was kneeling, I'd probably trip over him. And secondly, if he's kneeling before me without even knowing me, that tells me he'll kneel for anyone. I desire a slave who values his surrender and submission more highly than that.

Several Dominants I know feel the same; though not all Dominants view it that way and many enjoy when the submissive kneels before them in greeting. Like anything else in this lifestyle, it's all a matter of taste and the value you place on specific actions.

It should be understood that not all interactions with a Dominant will be physical, and definitely not all will be sexual in nature. Some Dominants are interested in submissives merely for their ability to provide good service, such as performing household chores, running errands, providing service in the form of accounting or other specialized skills. It is the service that then becomes the bases of the interaction between these two individuals.

Rewards for a good submissive may come in the form of acceptance and/or praise. One submissive I know loves to be able to crossdress while providing service and be accepted for who he is. For him, being able to cook and serve a meal in a dress and heels allows him to integrate that part of himself that he hides from the world. Imagine for a moment if you will what it feels like to be completely accepted for who you are. Finding one person who will not judge you or ridicule you is invaluable.

My favorite misunderstanding is the belief that you have to dress in leather or a slinky outfit in order to dominate another. The truth is, if you can't dominate a person in fufu slippers, jeans and a tee shirt with no makeup on, you couldn't dominate them looking flawless in full leather regalia. Though you my look better in leather, it doesn't immediately give you *Super Dominant Powers* or a burst of confidence. Nor does the leather help improve your skills at flogging or throwing a whip. Not to mention, cheap leather squeaks and good leather is really expensive!

And just for the record, throwing a whip around in three-inch heels is a pain in the ass (let alone four- or five-inch heels) especially when you bend down low to crack it against the slave's buttocks or back of his thighs and calves. Have you ever bent low in heels—not from the waist but actually bending your knees and going low—then tried to get up again without wobbling or worse yet, falling over? Imagine bending low repeatedly as you caress your slave's body with the whip or flogger.

No one stands in one place with perfect balance when using any BDSM toy. That would be like trying to kiss without moving your lips. And though we can all run in heels every now and then, a good scene can last anywhere from 30 minutes to a few hours. Heels will kill your feet by the end of play, and may even cause you to cut it shorter than you intended. I don't know about you, but I refuse to wobble about in heels. I value foot comfort. Yet even more than that, imagine how stupid you'd feel if you tipped over and fell on your butt while trying to whip someone—especially if it happened in public.

As for female slaves, they do look great in heels. And most male Dominants require that their submissives wear high heels. In their case, however, the restraints they're placed in helps with balance and besides, they're often hopping from one foot to the other or leaning forward on their toes. Not to mention the endorphins running through their body may help alleviate any immediate pain the shoes may cause. Yet mainly it's just that they're focused on other things going on and the demands placed on them and don't necessary have time for their foot woes. However, their feet will definitely ache the next morning, along with a few other places.

One Dominant man I met actually took his slave's comfort into consideration so greatly that he purchased a pair of cowboy heel thigh-high boots for her to wear, as opposed to the four-inch spiked ones most male Dominants prefer. When questioned by another male Dominant about it, he stated he valued his slave and planned to have her restrained for long periods of time, thus he wanted her as comfortable as possible so she'd "last longer" during their play.

Contrary to the myth that Dominants will accept any slave that darkens their doorway, or kneels before them, this is far from the truth!

Surprisingly, many male submissives—especially those new to the lifestyle—feel a female Dominant should immediately accept their surrender, and they actually become upset or belligerent when rejected even when the rejection is done respectfully. The male ego is the same in the BDSM lifestyle as in the vanilla realm!

As I previously mentioned, some males go to fetish clubs hoping to obtain a "free" Dominatrix session. You can easily spot these guys (and gals too). They're the guys that will go up to a group of women ask if they're dominant, and whether anyone wants to spank him. Kind of like the guy that goes to a table at a dance club and asks one woman after another to dance until he's rejected by all of them. Remember Dominants are selective and Masters are beyond discerning, as a lot of work goes into training a submissive and guiding them into the slave you desire. I don't want to say men are the only ones guilty of such behavior as some female submissives behave just as poorly; however, I have experienced more men acting this way.

It's important to notice the tone of voice the Dominant uses and when. A stern voice can be used to reprimand a disobedient slave. There's no yelling and screaming involved, just a very firm tone. Some Dominants use a softer more pleasant—even sensual—tone with their submissives, luring them into their powerful web. In fact, it's the softer tone a Sadist takes with a submissive that scares them the most, as the slave realizes that with a Sadist, it is when the Sadist is most quiet and thoughtful that they are creating the most physically torturous scenarios, calmly reaching for and embracing that sadistic side of themselves that they normally keep tightly leashed.

Much like the submissive that experiences a rush of endorphins as their body registers pain, a Sadist will experience a rush of adrenaline, which heightens their desire. Thus a Sadist engaging with a masochist creates a synergistic symbiotic connection between them wherein each receives what they desire. No, the slave doesn't necessarily have to be a masochist, the slave/submissive may simply accept the intensity because of their desire to please the Sadist.

I've known Masters/Mistresses who have stopped themselves from crossing the line with their submissive as they worked themselves up into a state of excitement that would push them into an area where their submissive would be taxed too highly either physically or mentally; thus, keeping the slave safe.

Some women experience a certain level of angst when embracing their Dominant or Sadistic side and may need some time and encouragement to embrace that aspect of themselves fully. It's not surprising really when we consider women are generally taught to be the "weaker sex" and not to assert themselves. They're seen as the bossy bitch who's on a power trip in the vanilla world when they behave as men are allowed to. Thus it's no wonder that when a woman first enters the lifestyle, she may often feel guilt, even shame, for her desire to dominate others. And for a Sadistic woman, she may even fear herself as she embraces those darker more animalistic *Thanatos* desires within herself.

For Latina women, there's also a cultural bias to struggle against, as machismo is spoon-fed into them from birth. The Latina will also struggle with religious beliefs that conflict with her desires. The Dominant Latina will stand apart from other Latinas who are submissive in nature. The Dominant Latina is a rarity— and the Sadistic one even more so.

Nonlifestyle friends will often accuse a Dominant woman of trying to emasculate her man or they will try to make her feel less than feminine and lacking in womanly virtues. This can make a Dominant/Sadistic woman feel isolated and cause her to turn against her very nature, hiding her desires from others, even from herself—keeping a tight leash on her desires. She may even fear she's "abnormal" or pathological and perhaps even dangerous to others. This feeling of isolation creates an internal struggle that is felt by many Dominant women until they find the acceptance of the BDSM community or like-minded individuals.

A Dominant woman may often experience a power struggle within her relationships and/or experience a constant "serial dating" pattern as she shuffles from one lover to another trying to find what she desires; and more importantly, a partner who will not be threatened by her dominance and assertive ways. This behavior is most often seen in women who haven't made the crossover into the BDSM realm or who don't see their actions as "dominant" in nature. They tend to date other dominant personalities looking for an "equal" relationship, when what they really seek is an alpha submissive or a sexual submissive.

Male Dominants don't seem to struggle with their dominant natures as much, as it's a societal norm and to some extent it's acceptable for them to be aggressive and assertive. However, they may still struggle with their sadistic or domineering desires, as society still views BDSM as a pathological affliction.

<u>Punishment</u>

One thing almost every Dominant will agree upon is the fact that you don't touch a slave/submissive when you are angry. Doing so would be akin to abuse, and the D/s and Master/slave relationships are based on mutual respect and even affection. Thus most Masters/Mistresses will dismiss their slaves for the night or send them to a corner while the Dominant cools off. Any punishment the submissive deserved will be decided upon and implemented when the Dominant is once more under control.

I knew a Sadist who purposely dropped her crop onto the floor as she reined in her anger and stepped away from her slave to avoid causing him injury. She then sat and watched him hang from the ceiling for over an hour. The slave was devastated for having caused his Master such "pain" that he cried silently fearing she would dismiss him. As I've mentioned, the emotional bonds in these relationships are phenomenal.

Unfortunately for the submissive, this "timeout" allows the Dominant to control their tempers and carefully calculate the punishment, determining the level of severity—including the level of pain that will be inflicted. For example, where the submissive typically receives a hard spanking during play time, this spanking may leave welts or even draw blood from a caning, causing major discomfort for days.

In the end, it's all about the character of the individual and his or her honor. A person who cannot be trusted in everyday situations and who has no control over their temper is not a Dominant to be trusted or played with, as their unpredictability makes them a risk to the submissive. It is why playing with a new Dominant for the first few times should always be done in public or after having thoroughly vetted the person (contacting their references and inquiring about the individual from other members of the community that you trust). Though not all individuals who are in the lifestyle engage in community events or are associated with public BDSM activities, those Dominants/Sadists who want to engage in higher levels of risk and edge play who refuse to learn how to keep their submissive safe aren't worth interacting with.

On a side note, it may also surprise you to learn that many Dominants (and submissives) will learn basic First Aid and CPR to ensure the safety of their partner.

The submissive/slave Perspective

There's a popular saying in the BDSM community that it's harder to kneel than it is to stand, and it takes more courage to be vulnerable than it does to control another. This is never more true than with a male submissive who is going against societal norms by surrendering to another—especially to a woman. He is often viewed as less masculine or macho, and the Dominant woman is accused of emasculating him. Yet, nothing is further from the truth!

In actuality, a submissive man can be more dangerous than a dominant one, especially when his Mistress/Master is threatened. Think of him as the knight who goes off to battle and destroys his enemies then returning to meekly kneel before his Lady. This submissive male doesn't stop being a macho man; he embraces all aspects of his nature, making him stronger.

It is the fear of being ostracized by other men and the fear of embracing their desire for submission that leads most men to identify as Dominant when first entering the BDSM community—until they feel comfortable enough within the community and with themselves that they can let go of their need to hide behind the façade of the Dominant male.

It is unfortunate that the submissive man's courage is often despised or openly ridiculed by Dominant men, who make no qualms about putting down submissive men or showing their disdain. However these same Dominant men think nothing wrong with a woman being submissive. I believe this duality is caused by the Dominant man's own internal fear of being seen as weak, a fear and perhaps prejudice that keeps him from offering his own submission. And it's not unheard of for a Dominant man to swear a Dominant woman to secrecy about his desire to be submissive to "just her" and only "in private."

For some slaves, the ability to serve is what brings peace to their lives. It is the feeling of total acceptance and acknowledgement they strive to gain in their lives. They love to show their appreciation and respect by working hard to be a good slave and attempt to anticipate the needs of their Master/Mistress. These slaves even correct their own behavior before it needs to be addressed or punished. These types of slaves are a treasure to have and are well-guarded once found.

As for submissive women, they're able to embrace the more feminine side of their nature as well as their desires to cater to their Dominant/Master/Mistress. She is able to give freely of herself, knowing her efforts and service will be greatly appreciated. In this era when feminist ideals often battle with submissive desires, a female submissive/slave may find herself ostracized by her feminist friends for what they perceive as her *subservient* or *backward* desires or she may receive a lot of undue objections for being of service to her Dominant as she dutifully performs her tasks of being the attentive "wife" and/or partner. Of course, men also fall prey to these objections from their friends, who will deem him "whipped." If they only knew how true it was!

Though the outside world may think a submissive suffers from little to no self-esteem or have a lack of personal power, the truth is far from it. In a way, submissive individuals are actually reclaiming their power and sharing it with others.

To dispel some rampant misconceptions, no slave/submissive is a doormat! Many are very strong, even dominant in their everyday vanilla interactions. Many have jobs where they are in charge or supervise others. They simply enjoy the ability to release their responsibilities and surrender to another individual they feel safe with. The need for surrender is strong in both men and women and though not all interactions with their Dominant are sexual in nature, I find that submissive women are used sexually more so than their male counterparts. This may be due to the physical dominance a woman exerts over a man, ensuring that he realizes that even his manhood *belongs to Her* and She'll use it when and as She desires. Also whereas male Dominants tend to be more comfortable being sexual in public, female Dominants often limit sexual interactions in public.

There's also a major difference between what a submissive/slave will engage in publicly versus private play. For instance, I've seen a male submissive withstand extreme physical torment in a public setting, including being whipped and having fire play and knife play performed on him while he was restrained. Yet, this same individual had a major panic attack during private play alone with his Mistress when all that was done to him was placing him in cuffs, something she had done to him numerous times in the past. The fear behind the panic attack was caused by the fact that in public he could cry out for help any time he choose to and the Dungeon Master would intervene; whereas in private, there was no one to come to his rescue.

As for sexual play, many female Dominants will save the more intimate aspects of their interactions with their partner for private times. This is not only due to their personal preferences but because having to get in and out of their more elaborate outfits is a bit more difficult. With submissive women, it's not uncommon and perfectly normal for them to be seen in the nude and be forced to orgasm in public or perform fellatio on their Dominant in public.

For sexual submissives, their desire to serve and be vulnerable is based solely on their sexual needs and that is where their submission ends, as in all other aspects of their lives and their interactions with their Dominant they are on equal footing and may even be dominant themselves. At times, you will have two Dominants who interact with each other successfully, outside the bedroom, because of the fact that one is a sexual submissive and therefore can give that aspect of themselves to the other, though you may find that in these types of relationships, the couple may engage a third party they share as the submissive to one or both of them.

Submissives adhere to the requirements of their Dominant! Every Dominant has their own requirements and protocols. Some will impose eye contact restrictions; prescribe a dress code, as well as specific protocols and rituals dictating how the submissive will greet them when arriving for a play scene or when they meet up at home, if they live together. These rituals and protocols reinforce the connection between the couples and are paramount to the relationship. They provide a sense of belonging and acceptance, even safety, for both.

For those submissives who are masochistic in nature, you may find that they tend to push and challenge their Dominants to receive more physical interactions, even punishments. This push may not even be a conscious behavior on their part. However it is their physical, emotional and even spiritual need to connect at that level of release and service to their Dominant that pushes them to tease and bring forth the more primal elements within their Dominant.

A masochist whose needs aren't being met will often act out, becoming rude, even disrespectful in hopes of being corrected and punished for his behavior. Unlike the slave who is in the relationship to be of service to his/her Dominant, the masochist can sometimes fall into the trap of being in service more for himself than to meet his Dominant's needs. For instance, being able to coax the sadistic aspects of his Dominant's nature is what he longs for; if he cannot, he will need another avenue to meet his desires. If he's in love with his Dominant and the Dominant isn't sadistic, the relationship may end or they will need to find a friend who is willing to serve their needs and inflict the sadism the slave/submissive craves.

For some masochists it's not so much that he's pitting himself against his Dominant, in the sense of taking as much as the Sadist/Dominant can provide, but that he's pushing against his own fears or need to be able to take more pain for his Dominant or himself, needing to be pushed to extremes and knowing he's safe and will be cared for afterward. It is when the slave is pushed to these extremes that the darker nature within him is released. It is during the release of his internal *beast* that he may become very aggressive, even feral with his Dominant, which creates its own delicious variations to the power exchange dynamics.

The Switches Perspective

Switches, those individuals both male and female, who straddle both sides of the whip and embrace various aspects of dominance and submission at varying times tend to fall into one category more so than the other when with a specific individual. For example: being either dominant or submissive depends on the other person's nature. If their partner is also switch, they will alternate as desired, even taking turns with who's the Dominant and who's the submissive.

The one benefit of being a switch is the ability to explore both sides of the spectrum—without guilt or shame—dominating another and submitting to them. However, if it's in your nature to be submissive (as with some sexual submissives), switching into

Dominant mode may be short-lived. Sometimes, these individuals are considered "Service Tops" or "service bottoms" depending on the service they offer.

Chapter 6

Relationships

Though they do resemble their vanilla cousins, Dominance and submission relationships differ based not only on the power exchange dynamics but on the level of communication and the willingness of each individual to open themselves up to their partner. This amazing mixture of acceptance, affection, exploration and vulnerability are the foundation of every healthy and long-lasting BDSM relationship.

The most amazing aspect of a Dominance and submission relationship isn't the erotic thrills or the "whips and chains" as most would believe—it's the communication. Dominants and submissives in a relationship speak about everything! Whereas most men and women entering into a vanilla relationship withhold information about their desires and sexual needs because they fear rejection or ridicule, in a power exchange relationship, these individual's most embarrassing desires, their fears of abandonment, their fears of failure and never being good enough, their need for love and most importantly what these issues look like are directly addressed. Granted the submissive typically opens him or herself up more so than the Dominant in this respect because let's face it who wants a wimpy Dominant. However it is through these revelations, this baring of the soul by both partners, that the foundation of the relationship is established.

This doesn't mean that the submissive or the Dominant won't decide somewhere along the line that this relationship isn't for them or that fears won't sometimes crop up and create obstacles; yet because of their willingness to be honest and bare their needs and in essence their soul and psyche to their partner, this couple reaches a level of intense emotional connection much faster and, I dare say, vastly deeper than conventional relationships.

The fact that these emotional and psychologically intense topics are open for discussion and reviewed makes these relationships more realistic and honest than the ones we come across where men and women hide behind a façade then wonder why things went wrong six months or two years or, god forbid, twenty years down the road.

I'm not saying that power exchange relationships are the best. What I am saying is, wouldn't it be wonderful if you could be completely open with your partner and not have to hide any aspects of yourself! To know that you're accepted completely despite your flaws or unconventional erotic desires.

Now just because Dominance and submission relationships are open it doesn't mean they don't have their own obstacles to overcome. The very fact that you're engaging in such emotional and psychological areas actually creates a whole host of different problems to deal with, such as insecurities, fears, abandonment issues, jealousy, dependency issues, and even timing/pacing of how the relationship should progress. Sound familiar? It should. These are the same issues that arise in vanilla relationships, only now they'll won't be overlooked or left to resolve themselves. Well, at least we hope that's what will happen.

I want to share some of the difficulties faced by Dominants and submissives in this lifestyle. Though these issues are not exclusive to either gender nor based on whether the woman is Dominant or submissive in the relationship's dynamics, I am presenting the examples from a Dominant woman/submissive man's perspective to help simplify things. Please remember nothing is set in stone. These examples can apply to Dominant men/submissive women's relationships as well. I'm just more comfortable with expressing it from the Dominant woman's point of view and where applicable, I've added the opposing view.

Difficulties Dominants Face

I've found that Dominant women face a unique obstacle in their relationships with submissive men that aren't mirrored in men-led relationships. The uniqueness comes from the internal battle Dominant women must face in order to accept themselves and become comfortable with their dominant desires.

In order to understand the struggles Dominant women face, it's essential to look at the societal and cultural norms we've been taught since birth. Let's face it, women have been taught to be subservient to men. We've been taught to care for them and put their needs and desires first; to give in to their more *logical* wisdom and vast experiences; to allow men to protect us since they're stronger and more capable of doing so than we are; and to conform to their dictates on how we should behave and interact with others. Of course, if we go against any of these expectations we won't be loved or accepted and will find ourselves alone, relegated to the spinster aunt or the single woman who will never have a family of her own and will die unwanted and unloved. Damn, isn't that depressing!

Sadly, we don't even realize we've bought into these beliefs since they've become unconsciously accepted. If you're not convinced of that, just think about how often you've felt guilty when you went against your male partner's needs or desires. We've been force-fed the roles of women and seen the prejudices and discrimination heaped upon those women who dare to become "powerful" in business or relationships. Women are thought of as bitches, power hungry whores, emotionally unbalanced, bipolar or worse for simply being tough and demanding (a dominant) whereas men in the same situation are thought of as dedicated and real "go getters."

Movies like *The Stepford Wives* set the standard for the "good wife," and Hollywood has depicted the Dominant woman as a leather-wearing whore who merely wants to eviscerate men while taking them for every penny they have. Or she's portrayed as a "*Mistress*" who can be used to satisfy a man's needs then easily discarded while the male returns to his cherished wife or girlfriend with whom he wouldn't dream of doing all those "dirty" sexual acts with.

Cultural biases also play a major role in a Dominant woman's self-acceptance. I remember always being the oddball in my family because I didn't conform to the subservience of women, which as a Latina, machismo was stuffed down my throat. Plus, the murals I drew on my walls as a teenager of men being flogged or tied deemed me the "emotionally troubled" girl of the family—something Dominant girls are often accused of.

Yet it's not only the Dominant woman who battles societal norms but the submissive man as well. Those unique men who long to surrender to a woman yet fear their surrender would be looked upon as weakness or inadequateness and lack of masculinity. These men and the women who love them, at times fear that their very submission would be despised by others and not seen for the strength it really is. Ironically, it is Dominant men who are guilty of discriminating against submissive men more so than vanilla women, who have a higher intolerance for their submissive brothers. Perhaps it is because the Dominant man fears he might be seen as weak merely by association, or he fears his own inner need for submission.

It's comical really when I think about all the Dominant men who strut about being "macho," declaring their superiority only to turn to Dominant women I know begging to surrender to them—and swearing the women to secrecy, denying they've ever considered it before: they forget women *talk* and share information. I'm in no way ridiculing these Dominant men, merely pointing out that the sexual scale Alfred Kinsey developed to show the variation of sexual desire in human beings should have a counterpart—*a Kinky Scale*—if you will, which would delineate the variation of dominance and submission in men and women.

There's a saying in the Leather community that it takes more strength to kneel before another than to stand before them—submissive men in particular demonstrate this. But just because they are submissive doesn't mean they won't rally to the defense of their women or have alpha personalities. Envision the knight who slaughters his enemy by day then willingly kneels before his Lady at night, surrendering all to her—that's a true submissive man.

Some believe that you can't have love in a Master/slave or Dominant/submissive relationship because the affection and love you feel for the submissive will limit your desire to punish them when necessary or correct inappropriate behavior. I find this has merits on both sides. Yes, there is an underlying fear that your slave/submissive might decide to leave you if you punish them or that they'll lose affection for you; yet, isn't the fact that you correct them, that you value them enough to punish inappropriateness, proof of your affection? If you didn't correct their behavior or punish them appropriately doesn't that show that you really didn't care? Just as with anyone you love, family member, friend or lover, pointing out their shortcomings may cause a fall-out yet it is those very instances that show you the character of the person and helps you decide if you really want to remain in a relationship with them.

For women, this issue of discipline can at times create its own internal struggle. How do you discipline a man without damaging his psyche or slamming up against his ego?

In the vanilla realm women withhold sex and/or kick the man out of bed, relegating him to the couch or as we affectionately call it *the doghouse*—or impose some other emotional withholding. Within the power exchange, *the doghouse* has a whole different meaning. And though I've previously mentioned various forms of punishment, such as spanking, whipping, and humiliation, the fact is that all of these punishments come with a degree of angst for some Dominant women, especially Latinas and women from cultures who need to see their men as "strong." However if you don't punish him, you are robbing him of your affection and dominance since every "naughty boy" deserves to be spanked! Plus, it is these punishments that show you his true surrender—his acceptance of your dominance over him and his desire to live a female-led relationship. It is at these times, Dominant women need to embrace their own female dominance and hold onto their belief that their male submissive will turn toward them and not run away once the punishment is over. The only analogy I can think of here is the mother with her child. You have to punish them when they're bad and accept the fact that they (the submissive) may not like you for a little while, but he'll return to loving you as soon as his pride stops hurting.

Another issue I find some Dominant women struggle with is their own vulnerability and fears. This struggle isn't unique to Dominant women as some Dominant men struggle with it as well, and I daresay, Dominant men struggle with it more so, because women are allowed to be emotional and reveal their fears and vulnerabilities whereas men aren't.

Because of the uniqueness of their designated roles within the D/s relationship, Dominants are apprehensive of revealing their fears, their insecurities, and their feelings of inadequacy to their submissives/slaves because of their concern that these valid emotional will be perceived as "weaknesses." Let's face it, Dominants are supposed to be the "strong" ones. We're not supposed to be wimpy! And yes, I have known of relationships, especially female-led relationships, where the submissive male left because he felt the woman was not "dominant" enough because she cried in front of him.

At times, the needs of the dominant are overlooked or brushed under the rug so to speak because of this very belief; Dominants aren't allowed moments of weakness. It's like seeing Mom cry for the very first time and fearing the world will come to an end, since she's human and not the *superbeing* you thought her to be.

In order to overcome these very fears, it's essential that the Dominant find support in friendships with other Dominants who can help her (or him) address these fears and insecurities, since discussing them with a submissive is actually counterproductive to the relationship. It's the equivalent of using your partner as your therapist or as your best girlfriend. Sure you want to be able to share everything with your submissive (your partner); however, getting a good perspective on what you want to say and making sense of your feelings before you address them with your submissive/slave is always best. Without this support, your D/s relationship will suffer or dissolve altogether—or worse, become vanilla and leave you both unhappy and unfulfilled, wondering what happened and feeling like there's something missing.

Another issue some Dominant women face is their desires to have a strong powerful alpha male beside them who can be domineering in his everyday life and within his interactions with others yet surrender only to her. We've been raised on this concept since infancy. Cinderella. Snow White. Rapunzel. Men coming to our rescue. Who wouldn't treasure that? Someone always on our side! Someone strong and fearless willing to champion our cause and battle the dragon. And yet, here we are—Dominant women—wanting that very same hero to kneel before us and allow us to whip him, punish him, even make him cry out in surrender and not be seen as monsters ourselves.

There are even sexually dominant only women who desire their men to be submissive to her only in the bedroom and have him be the alpha male in every other aspect of his/their lives. We previously spoke about these individuals—the sexual submissives. In this case, the Dominant woman is turned on by the fact that her submissive/slave is strong and self-assured. She wants him to call her on "her crap" when necessary—in a respectful manner of course. To make her feel like she belongs to another and is treasured and cherished. This feeling of *ownership,* which is regulated to slaves and submissives, is a way of feeling loved. In these relationships, it is the Dominant's responsibility to teach her slave how to offer that level of assertiveness in a manner that will not disrupt the power exchange or the balance within the D/s relationship. As a Dominant friend once shared with me, she taught her slave how to run his hand caressingly over her back, up to her neck, only to bury his hand in her hair and pull her head back to deliver a demanding kiss that left them both longing for more and served to feed her desire to share her dominance with him.

Another type of dominance is the Dominant women (and dominant men) who want to have their submissive/slave to use them harshly. These Dominant women are considered sadomasochistic in their orientation. They enjoy being whipped or flogged or tied up and used sexually. Unlike the example I gave above about the dominant man who swears the Dominant woman to secrecy about his desire to surrender to her, in this instance there is no actual desire to surrender. This Sadomasochistic woman (or man) merely desires her alpha slave to share his *beast* with her. To have her slave surrender even the *beast* within him to her needs, her desires. To show her slave that despite the darker shadows of his nature, she would accept him and allow him to use them on her (not against her) for their mutual pleasure. Unlike the male Dominant who wanted to kneel before a woman, this Dominant wants to unleash the *beast* within her slave/submissive not so she can kneel before him, but to play with him and tame him to her specifications.

It's imperative to understand that dominance runs the gambit of light to extreme. Among these extremes there is a unique category of men and women who enjoy the emotional and physical extremes and the more intense levels of edge play within the power exchange. These individuals are known as Sadists. Ironically, Sadistic women are often accused of hating men because they enjoy putting their submissives through more stringent and physical interactions than merely sensual/sexual ones. The irony is in the fact that sadistic men who engage in similar activities with female submissives are readily accepted. Another example of gender biases even within so liberated a community.

One female Sadist gave this response when asked what she gets out of being sadistic to a man, "There's this feeling of peace that comes over me when I push my slave to that level of surrender—where I push us both to giving more than we ever imagine possible. It's when I stand before him, knowing that with one more word—one more strike— I can push him off the cliff and shatter him—perhaps shatter us both—and instead of him running away from me or calling me names and telling me I'm insane, he clings to me, demanding more, plunging us both over that cliff and holding onto me as we fall, trusting in me to be there for him afterwards. At that moment, there's a silence that enters my soul and I feel complete. I feel the world stop and only we exist. At that moment, I want nothing more than to hold onto him and keep him safe…and love him forever."

Yes, even the Sadistic woman doubts herself at times and struggles with societal norms, wondering if she's the monster and man-hater some deem her. I believe, the Sadist more so than any other Dominant woman has a harder time finding the right submissive for her; someone who isn't there just to get off on pain and/or humiliation but who is willing to surrender all he is, then stand proudly beside her—or before her when others threaten.

It is finding these men in tarnished armor that a Dominant woman longs for. Why tarnished armor? Well, the "shiny" ones are why too vanilla for a Dominant woman.

As for Dominant men, they often do not face the same emotional turmoil as Dominant women since their dominant natures are accepted based solely on their gender.

However, I have known many Dominant men who struggle with their internal desires to be sadistic with women or to give voice to their submissive needs. And though I've not discussed the struggles of Switches (those individuals who enjoy both sides of the whip), I've found that these individuals tend to fall into one category moreso than the other, therefore the struggles they face lies within that particular category.

Difficulties submissives Face

Female submissives tend to thrive in their submission and are more readily acceptable since we live in a patriarchal society where women are expected to take the subservient role.

In contrast there are the alpha females and the Feminist who struggle with their desire to serve because it goes against their nature of being in control or their values and fight for women's suffrage. Then again, let's not overlook those women and men who are only sexually submissive and are in control of their lives, careers and families. With these individuals, submission is a desire they practice in limited circumstances. Don't get me wrong. I am in no way stating that they are not submissive in their hearts, but that they choose with whom and when to be submissive, in what manner, and to what degree.

It's important to remember that though male and female submissives both share the desire to serve, they do not face the same prejudices from gender counterparts. Dominant men will often ridicule and degrade submissive men. As I mentioned previously, I believe this has to do with that dominant man's fear of seeing himself portrayed in the submissive man; the same prejudice and fear I notice in heterosexual men against their gay brothers. At times this prejudice may be unconscious on the Dominant's part. After all, he's been raised to feel superior and to look upon other's who don't measure up to him as weak. Dominant men who are confident in themselves don't display this inappropriate behavior.

The most significant struggle some submissive men face is an internal one with their very soul-deep desire to surrender. Everything they've learned teaches them that they should be the ones in control, the ones who are strong, the ones to protect and the ones who are to be served; and yet they long to surrender, to allow their loved one to use them in any manner they desire whether physically or sexually. The male submissive longs to give up his very essence in service to his Dominant so that he may derive pleasure from bringing join to Her. Even being forced to engage in sexual activities he would not usually perform, would be acceptable because they are done according to his Dominant's demands and desires.

Ironically, it is when men (and women) are provided with everything they desire that they run from their Dominant! It is the fear of when fantasy becomes reality that makes them flee despite their vows of commitment and desire to surrender. Or they merely desired the fantasy because they wanted the erotic thrill they read about or saw in a movie. Sadly, these emotionally deficient men ruin it for the rest of the male submissives who long to find their Dominant.

Some alpha males want to surrender to a Dominant yet have no desire to be subservient to her nor be in a female-led relationship. These men experience their own internal struggles as they battle their domineering natures while attempting to surrender to another. Often, these men do not realize they are merely sexual submissives and therefore struggle with themselves and their Dominants. Finding the right degree of surrender is essential for these individuals, both male and female. They would do well with a sexual Dominant partner. (The sexual Dominant is someone who enjoys the power exchange yet may not adhere to the various protocols required from a slave/submissive and prefers a more equalitarian relationship with her slave.)

Another struggle for men is their pride. This often works against them as they struggle with their need to surrender and the demands placed upon them. Sometimes, submissives will dissolve their relationship because of these demands, only to return a few weeks or months later wanting to "try again." The major downfall I see with this behavior and way of expressing their fear is that they will continuously leave the relationship, causing heartache and mistrust.

Though it is the submissive's right to leave any relationship whenever they desire; in the same vein, it is their responsibility to trust in their Dominant to help them through their fears and to hold strong despite those fears. This shows character and dedication. If you have a slave/submissive who's constantly running, why chase! You'd be better off finding one who will stick around even when things go bad—just as you would expect in a vanilla relationship.

Yes, the same can be said about a Dominant who leaves when things get tough. There's an adage that goes like this, "everyone knows how to be a good Dominant until they have a slave of their own." The same can be stated in reverse about a submissive. The bottom line in any relationship whether vanilla or D/s is communication, love, and establishing, then maintaining, the foundation it is built upon so that it may thrive for years to come.

Types of Relationships

There are many kinds of Dominance and submissive relationships. Not all are based on sexual interactions. Some relationships are merely protective in nature. These include mentoring, coaching, protection, service-oriented, play only, and of course fully owned.

A protection-based relationship is one in which the Dominant offers his or her protection to a new submissive or to a slave who is new or who recently lost their collar (was dismissed from their prior relationship). In this instance, the Dominant is acting as a big brother/big sister per se, providing emotional support and even screening potential play partners for the submissive/slave. In this way, the submissive/slave has someone they can depend on to help them through this emotional crisis.

In a mentoring-based relationship, the individuals can be of either gender and embrace either side of the power exchange continuum. For instance, mentoring can occur between two Dominants, two submissives or even a Dominant and submissive. It may surprise you to discover that often it is the submissive who trains an inexperienced Dominant in the ways to use her/his slave. Who better to learn from than the one experiencing it! However, that said, a Dominant learns from another Dominant how to embrace their darker needs and the various ways in which to exert their dominance upon their submissive. It's also essential to have peer-based relationships, as Dominant and submissive emotional needs and struggles are not the same and you cannot always share certain fears or emotional struggles with each other. That would be the equivalence of a parent asking a child for advice.

For instance, a Dominant who fears their darker nature would either scare their submissive with their revelations as they tried to make sense of it since, let's face it, the submissive is the one being used physically. Thus imagine a Dominant telling the submissive I want to cane you till you bleed, but I'm afraid I won't stop there. It would make anyone doubt their partner and perhaps even run away. The same can be said about the Dominant who feels guilty for exerting their power. Though the submissive can reassure them and say, "But I love when you control me," those words don't serve to alleviate the guilt. However another Dominant can share their struggles with embracing their power and how they overcame the guilt and/or fear of sharing the darker—*Thanatos*—side of their nature.

The same is true of a Dominant trying to reassure a submissive that their surrender is totally natural and appreciated. It is learning from their peer, another slave, which will assist the individual to embrace that aspect of their nature completely.

Some power exchange relationships have nothing to do with sex and in fact there may be no physical interaction between the two individuals. These types of relationships are called service-oriented. The service may be in the form of a deed or act. For example, the slave/submissive may clean the Dominant's apartment, do their bookkeeping, run errands for them, or cook their meals. The satisfaction for the slave/submissive in these types of relationships is in the ability to be of service, to make the life of the Dominant less stressful. To assist the Dominant in finding joy in their life this in turn brings joy to the submissive. These acts of submission are not reimbursed by a monetary exchange. In fact, the slave/submissive would probably be offended if money were offered as their pleasure is in the ability to have someone to take care of. From the Dominant's perspective, being able to share their control with another even in this platonic manner is fulfilling.

Play only relationships are those in which there is no sexual interaction between the Dominant and the submissive. In these relationships, the play remains physical in nature, however sexual intercourse is not part of it. This doesn't mean that the slave would not be naked before the Dominant or that their breasts or genitalia were not used during their interactions, but that sexual acts would not be engaged in. Thus a play only relationship may include breasts and genital torture but not actual penetration.

Also play only relationships can be part of a power exchange relationship, where one of the individuals in the relationship is unable to or unwilling to participate in D/s activities. For instance, a Dominant may offer his submissive to another Dominant to whip because that is something that he/she doesn't enjoy doing but wants to give his submissive the experience. In this instance, the other Dominant would whip the submissive while his/her Master/Mistress watched, leaving the aftercare to the slave's owner.

There are also play only relationships where the individual's partner is not into Dominance and submission; however it allows the individual to appease their internal desire for the Power Exchange. Also when the Dominant or the submissive isn't physically able to engage in such activities, their partner may allow them to do so.

Though I find the majority of individuals engaging in the BDSM community full of honor and respect, it is the males and females, both Dominant and submissive, who engage in BDSM activities without the consent of their vanilla partner that I find despicable, as essentially they are "cheating" regardless of whether their interactions are sexual in nature or not. The fact is they are engaging in an emotional connection with another individual, while hiding the fact that they're married, engaged, or dating vanilla and creating an emotional connection with someone they have no intention of honoring completely. There are basically dabbling in the BDSM community for a sexual thrill or to point and giggle.

Full ownership relationships—Dominance and submission, Master and slave relationships—are based on an underlying foundation of trust and communication, as without these two essential factors no BDSM relationship could survive. Each BDSM relationship is unique. Each expands and grows with time, solidifying itself along the way as it overcomes obstacles and emotional turmoil. In order for any D/s relationship to survive and grow, it needs the support of like-minded individuals. This is why I recommend couples engaged in D/s relationships join their local BDSM organizations and/or participate in the various workshops available to enhance their relationships. It is also why I created the Dominance and submission Therapy/Mentoring model, which takes into consideration the uniqueness of interacting on a power exchange platform and helping couples embrace their nature and enhance their relationship by reinforcing the BDSM foundation.

Of course, no discussion is complete without discussing Internet-based BDSM relationships. Yes, I do believe these relationships hold a plethora of emotions and can be a wonderful start to any long-lasting relationship. It is the "mail order bride" equivalent of the 18th and 19th century. (Or male order as I like to say.) However, if the individual you're interacting with is not willing to meet within three months—six at the maximum—then cut your losses and run as fast as you can from that relationship, since you will be wasting your energies on someone who will never commit and who will find something—anything—wrong with you once he/she does meet you face-to-face. This is what always happens when fantasy becomes reality!

It's devastating to learn that the person you've been interacting with for so many months has lied or upon meeting you decides they no longer feel the same as they did when you were interacting over the phone or via computer. Thus it's always best to set a time limit for these types of interactions unless you're happy sharing your life with someone you will never meet.

I always tell women and men who come to me for therapy or coaching/mentoring suffering from a broken heart or emotional pain due to these relationships that the time they spent was not in vain. During these interactions they grew and learned what they desired in a relationship and strengthened their ability to engage with others in such. Now they merely need to take that knowledge into a more fulfilling relationship, one in which the person will honor and cherish the gifts they bring, whether those gifts are their Dominance or their submission.

As with any other relationship, there are no guarantees. There is only what you put into it and what you get out of it. Let's hope that both are the very best.

Chapter 7

Those deliciously wicked *Things* we do!

Now that we've discussed the fundamentals and the psychological aspects of Dominance and submission, let's put it all together to discover the emotional connections associated with all those deliciously wicked and sinfully erotic activities.

The essential thing to keep in mind when dealing with BDSM is to allow yourself to become what I like to call the *sensual scientist.* This is where you explore the mind-body connection. From the Dominant's perspective it's about allowing them to explore and derive sensual and sexual pleasure from what they do to their slave, thus exploring the physical and sexual aspects of control as well as pleasure and pain. From the submissive's perspective, it's about being of service and letting go of their inhibitions and fears in order to be vulnerable to and with another, surrendering all they are.

Here's another way to look at the dynamics of a D/s relationship. Imagine for a moment that the Dominant is the sea and the submissive is a sailboat; what amazing things they will experience together as they take their journey. The various storms along the way. the amazing silence that brings peace to the soul. Even all the creatures they'll discover along their path, both big and small—adventures both frightening and inspiring. Though it may not always be smooth sailing, it will be a new exploration of the core self each time, as the individuals learn something new about themselves and each other.

There is no way I will be able to cover every possible scene and toy, however I want to provide you with several scenarios and a little insight into how these implements feel on the body and the psychological effect they have on both the Dominant and the submissive.

Whenever possible, try these toys and/or activities on yourself. Allow yourself to experience the excitement or fear or whatever emotion that crops up. Be sure to address all the senses—sight, sound, taste, touch, smell—as well as the mental-psychic connection, which is the heart of the BDSM experience.

Before I forget, I want to address a little concern; if you're on a budget, many of the tools needed or implements used can be easily purchased at a local hardware store or made from items purchased there. Home Depot or "Dom-Depot" as the community tends to call it, carries almost everything you'll need, including rope and, of course, wood, so you can make your very own St. Andrews Cross to tie your slave up to—or have your Dominant tie you up.

To simplify things, as I don't know if you are Dominant or submissive, I will address the examples and exercises below as if I were mentoring a Dominant. Performing these exercises whether you're Dominant or submissive will help you get a little more understanding into the emotional connections made by both individuals.

As we discuss the various objects and implements used during scenes or merely to enhance a couple's less formal interactions, it's crucial to remember that everything will feel different to each individual depending on their vulnerability and the comfort of their position, as well as the exposure the activity provides. Thus what someone is willing to do in the privacy of their own home, they may not be willing to do in public. The reverse is also true, as the more dangerous edgy interactions they may be willing to endure in public (with a Dungeon Master or others able to immediately come to their rescue), they may not engage in privately when there is no one to aide them. The vulnerability they experience in private with their Dominant as opposed to the exhibitionistic experience they had in public will also put a different emotional spin on the interactions.

Another thing to keep in mind is the feeling of vulnerability a person experiences based on arm placement and their inability to move about. For example, having your arms tied behind your back will provide one sensation, while having them tied over your head will bring another. It goes without saying that having a submissive's arms tied behind their back and then incorporating their feet (like being hog-tied) will increase the submissive's level of vulnerability. However, this position will interfere and limit which areas of the body will be available to the Dominant. For example, you wouldn't be able to use the slave's buttocks, yet his/her genitals would be exposed.

To give you a taste of what this feels like, please play along with me for a moment and notice the different sensations you experience in each example I provide. Notice for yourself what feels comfortable, what feels threatening, what makes you sigh with boredom and what revs you up. Of course, your submissive doesn't have to be physically tied: the real surrender comes when the Dominant mentally binds the submissive, not needing ropes or restraints because the submissive knows that their surrender would please their Master/Mistress, thus in essence becoming the rope that binds them.

A little taste of wickedness

For each example, hold the position for at least two to three minutes. Use an hourglass or loud egg timer to keep track of time. This will help you get the psychological feel, as well as the physical. Let the sensual scientist take notice of your heart rate, your breathing, whether you quickly jumped from one activity to the next or whether you lingered in one more so than the others. Is there anticipation? Excitement? Nervousness? Embarrassment? Notice for yourself if you enjoyed the position or if your mind was busy thinking of different things you could in each position. This is just step one of all the various ways you can add to the mental and physical aspects of Dominance and submission and power exchange interactions in your life.

If you first perform these exercises alone, try them with someone instructing you to do them. Note the difference and the vulnerability factor associated with each. If you really want to get a gold star in your sensual scientist role, explore the difference between a man providing instructions as opposed to a woman. You will notice the dynamics will shift. Take note of which activities you rebelled against and which you accepted easily.

Once you've taken instruction (been the submissive), take control—be the Dominant! Have a friend or lover perform these tasks for you. Exploring both sides of these exercises will help you analyze the internal connections they might feel.

If you can, use a full-length mirror to enable you to see yourself in each position. It's not only the feelings and internal connections made that push the individual into subspace or Domspace, it's viewing themselves in that position, even imagining what onlookers might see, which pushes them over the edge. Remember that the mind drives the body. It is the seduction and capture of the mind that will send the person into the mindset of surrender or dominance, to even be seduced or enticed to accept more pain. Whatever else you need to get you ready to explore, do it. Allow yourself to explore these positions to the fullest.

Don't forget to add a little music to the background. You'll be amazed how the tempo and the words will affect your mindset. Even the emotional connections associated with the type of music you choose can change how you feel. Just as you create a romantic ambiance, create a D/s one. This is part of setting the scene. When performing your exercises, do the same to provide yourself with the fullest possible effect.

Dare I mention the added sense of vulnerability you will feel should these exercises be done in the nude?

Exercise #1
Stand up and place your hands at the small of your back. Right palm over left. Fingers flat. Thumbs touching. Press your shoulders back and stand up straight and proud. Your eyes should be straight ahead. If someone is standing before you, you should not make eye contact. Correct yourself every time you do. If you're alone, place an object (like a statue) in front of you to

represent a person; notice how often your eyes involuntarily drift to it.

Exercise #2
Place your hands behind your neck, pushing your elbows out so they are parallel to your shoulders. Stand with your feet shoulder width apart. Again use the eye-contact restriction, unless the other person instructs you to look at them. You may find that the eye-contact restriction allows you to distance yourself a bit from the experience; however making that eye contact could make you feel a bit giddy, nervous, shy, embarrassed, exhilarated, etc.

Exercise #3
Place your hands over your head, extending them upward as if they were tied to the ceiling, with your wrists together. Legs spread shoulder width apart. It'll amaze you to realize that if you spread your feet another two to three inches apart, the feeling of vulnerability will increase. And yet, notice that nothing new has been added. You're in the same position as before. Now close your eyes and let your head fall back. Don't forget to breathe. (Something a Dominant is often reminding a submissive to do. Funny how they forget to do that. It's a normal human habit to hold your breath when excited or in nervous anticipation.)

***

Remember to notice your reactions. Your breathing. Your body. Are your hands sweating? Are you cold? Notice your thoughts even though you are just doing these simple exercises to get a feel for what you or a submissive might experience. Are you finding yourself trying to distance yourself emotionally from the sensations of vulnerability? Are you telling yourself, "This is silly" or are you becoming excited, allowing your mind to wonder what could happen next? Have you slipped into the Dominant role and started to think about all those deliciously wicked things you can do to one another in each position?

Give yourself permission to experience everything. Later you can analyze it and rehash all the nuances and reflect on all those feelings you experienced.

Even not feeling anything is something!

Exercise #4
Kneel and place your hands in the positions mentioned above. Again, notice how each position creates its own emotional connection with nothing more significant than the placement of the hands, the eye contact or restriction, and even head placement. This emotional connection will change if a blindfold is incorporated, especially if there are others in the room with you. Blindfolds are a wonderful tool to help a submissive focus on just the Dominant and/or just the experience the Dominant desires to share. The blindfold also increases their feeling of vulnerability.

Exercise #5
Get down on all fours. Hold yourself steady. After two to three minutes, let your shoulders drop to the floor while you push your buttocks upward into the air. Each position creates its own sensation, its own sense of vulnerability.

Now lie on the floor on your belly and reach back to grab your ankles. Notice the feelings that arise—vulnerability—rebellion—each person is different. What parts of your body are exposed? Is it comfortable? Difficult to breathe? Lift your head up and maintain that position for two minutes. Can you?

***

I can keep going with various positions but you get the picture. As a sensual scientist, exploring these positions for yourself will provide you with a realistic idea of what body parts and areas are exposed and vulnerable. Notice what's visible and what's exposed to the eye and/or an instrument/toy that might be used.

It goes without saying that performing these basic activities dressed would be vastly and erotically different than if performed in the nude with someone instructing you. Plus you'll also experience a different level of vulnerability, resistance, rebellion and so on depending on whether the person instructing/observing is male or female, friend or lover—or one of each.

Toys and Instruments
for Delicious Torment

I want to address the instruments, toys, and props used during play and some of the various aspects associated with them; to give you a little flavor of what it would be like to experience and experiment with them.

You can view various versions of these items online. My two favorite websites/stores are Mr. S Leather www.mr-s-leather.com and Stormy Leather www.stormyleather.com.

Mr. S Leather caters toward the male and Leather Men community. They have the best quality leather and products on the market for both men and women. They also have extraordinary equipment to feast your wickedly creative mind upon. Indulge your wicked imagination about the various possibilities based on the equipment you find on their site or many others. It's like a Dominant candy store!

Stormy Leather caters more toward women, offering lots of great corsets. If you're looking for plus size women's apparel and ideas for clothing, Hips & Curves www.hipsandcurves.com caters to plus size women and carries a great selection of reasonably priced corsets and sexy lingerie. Feel free to research these websites to view the items I describe below.

Blindfolds

Good blindfolds have a fur lining, which ensures the slave cannot peek by raising their heads and looking between the gaps that inferior blindfolds leave just between the eyes and the bridge of the nose. Also, the fur will cushion the delicate skin of the eyelids, creating a feeling of comfort, which lures the slave into further surrender.

The beauty behind blindfolds is that it immediately helps intensify anything you do. It is a Dominant's best friend. The submissive will become hyper vigilant and aware of his/her surroundings. Their hearing becomes attuned to every small noise. Their heartbeat automatically accelerates. Their apprehension will increase, as they try to determine what the Dominant will do next. Plus if the Dominant moves away from the slave and stays quiet or merely observes, the slave often has an intense reaction—anything from feeling anxious, frustrated, fearful, tearful, etc. Some submissives/slaves may even feel a sense of abandonment if the Dominant remains quiet for too long and react with anger, even aggression, and demand to be set free.

The Dominant can let them struggle with these emotions, testing them, allowing the slave/submissive to work through it themselves. However, it's never good to leave a submissive unattended. Just like with a candle, the slave/submissive can melt quickly or burn the house down. The Dominant can alleviate some of the submissive's fear by occasionally speaking or touching the slave softly, then leaving them to their silence once more. Psychologically, this creates an intense effect, as most individuals aren't used to sitting in silence. Don't be surprised if the slave/submissive cries or becomes very emotional.

Imagine the shock the submissive will experience if they thought they were alone and they carried on a verbal conversation with themselves—out loud. Perhaps they displayed their anger or resentment at the Dominant for "leaving them alone." Would the Dominant punish them for it or chuckle at the behavior, startling the slave?

When playing physically with whips or other impact instruments, the blindfolds allow the submissive to feel the impact more intensely, as they have nowhere to go but into their minds and their bodies. Using blindfolds pushes the slave into subspace more quickly, especially during psychological play such as fear play and mind fucks. Therefore, if the Dominant wants the slave to last longer in those situations and endure more, he shouldn't use the blindfold or should remove it after a while. Eye-contact restriction will work in lieu of the blindfold, and you can reinforce the restriction by swatting the submissive if they don't obey.

Blindfolds are extremely effective when conducting *Mind Fucks* (head trips), as you want to create a sense of fear and time/place distortion. You can even introduce other players who may or may not touch the slave. However, the slave won't know for sure who is doing the touching since he/she can't see. The Dominant can also disguise one hand in a vampire glove or a latex one, creating other sensations. And if you were in a hotel room, the Dominant could order room service and torment the slave with the idea of being seen by the wait staff when dinner is delivered.

One couple I know was traveling in from different states and meeting up at a hotel in Chicago, where the Dominant was hosting an event. As the slave was due to arrive first, they arranged that his Mistress would call him once her plane arrived and she was on her way to the hotel. The slave was instructed to be waiting in the room, kneeling in the corner, naked, his back to the door, with a blindfold on.

When the Dominant arrived at the hotel loaded with packages, the bellhop insisted on helping her take the packages into the room and bypassed her in his overzealous attempt at being helpful. As he entered the room and placed the packages down, he looked up to see the slave quietly kneeling in the far corner, naked, with his arms behind his back, and a blindfold over his eyes. It took the bellhop a moment to get over his shock before he quickly finished unloading the packages from the trolley and placing them in the room. The bellhop left with a huge tip and an interesting story to tell.

Though this was definitely not planned, the Dominant of course used the situation to her advantage, teasing the slave about being seen naked by a stranger. The Dominant then incorporated this embarrassing situation (for both of them, though she would never admit it to him) into actual play and rewarded the slave for not breaking his protocol and maintaining the required position, despite his shock at the bellhop's unplanned inclusion. She also incorporated a deliciously wicked mind fuck throughout their stay at the hotel, as she'd tease him about exactly which bellhop had witnessed his surrender.

As you can see, blindfolds are a must-have!

Gags

Gags of any type are interesting little torture devices all their own. On the one hand, it makes a slave feel more vulnerable, because no one will be able to hear him/her scream; yet on the other hand, it prevents the Master/Mistress from hearing her slave cry out or beg for mercy or respond coherently.

There are many different gags available, from the popular ball gag to the more erotic penis-shaped gags. There are even gags with phallic shapes on the outside, which the Dominant can then use for their own pleasure. There are dental gags that hold the mouth wide open to allow for oral penetration. The only bad part about these is they cause the slave to drool. Unless you enjoy that look, it's not the best gag choice. Of course, the Dominant would never dream of using their slave's unavoidable drooling against them, would they?

Because their ability to communicate with the Dominant is impaired, the submissive must be provided with another form of communication. Placing a yo-yo in their hand, with the string tied around their finger to prevent it from rolling away or creating a possible tripping hazard is a good option. This will allow the slave to release the yo-yo if they are in distress and/or if they want to use their safeword or for whatever other reason they might need to capture their Master's attention. Having the yo-yo tied to the finger prevents the Master/Mistress from having to search for it. The Master can then attend to the slave's needs, reroll the yo-yo, place it once more in the slave's hand, and start anew. The yo-yo also acts as a warning device for poor circulation if the submissive forgets to bring such information to the Dominant's attention.

Restraints
There is a wide selection of restraints. Each will produce its own effect as well as psychological connection. Rope has one effect. Metal another. Some individuals may feel comfortable with minimal rope restraints, others will need total immobility.

You will find a different emotional connection with rope bondage as opposed to metal restraints. The only explanation I can think of is that metal restraints have the psychological perspective of being permanent and unbreakable, plus it has the additional factor of added weight on the submissives wrists and/or ankles and on the body, if you encased them in chains. And perhaps with ropes, there's an unconscious belief that you can bite through them or cut through them somehow if necessary, where you can't do that with metal handcuffs. There's also the punitive aspect of handcuffs and the feeling of being "caught," just like a criminal. Rope does not have the same punitive association.

There are various restraints specifically built to take comfort into consideration. Many of the leather cuffs used for restraints are fur-lined. This aids the submissive in remaining in them longer. Really good quality suspension cuffs are built with a piece of metal that the submissive can grab onto while being suspended, giving the slave the illusion of control and serving to help take weight off the wrists.

Some submissives are only interested in bondage and do not need any further interaction, as the feeling of vulnerability from having their bodies immobilized is erotic enough to them and they neither want nor need any further stimulation. For these individuals, it is the bondage itself that sends them into subspace— a submissive's feeling of euphoric release.

<u>Rope Bondage</u>

There are various levels of rope bondage and degrees of expertise. Look up Midori or Steve Speliotis, and you'll discover some beautiful depictions of rope bondage. The most important aspect of this technique is its intimacy. When you are tying someone in intricate knots and positions, you are spending hours with them—literally. This is one of the reasons submissives love to be tied up in rope. They literally have their Master/Mistress' complete attention and focused on them. Some experienced bondage players can maneuver the body into intricate designs while still keeping the submissive comfortable.

Rope bondage creates its own level of intimacy and play. I once watched a woman place a man into an intricate rope bondage from start to finish. I was fascinated by the interchange between this Mistress/slave couple as well as the finesse of what she was doing. The end result was that she created a human chandelier, complete with little tea lights/votives strategically placed along his arms and legs along with hanging crystals that she placed in various areas hanging from the rope. However, it was the connection between them that was so sensual and romantic at once. Her soft words of encouragement while she artistically arranged the rope around him, the expression of trust and affection on his face as he looked up at her or nuzzled his cheek against her shoulder as he sought to connect with her or her palm every now and then wanting to feel closer to her was breathtaking to watch.

Predicament bondage is another form of rope play. The Master/Mistress ties the slave in such a way that moving one area of their body will create movement and discomfort in another area of their body, creating a live marionette. For instance, the right hand is tied across the body so that it is resting against the slave's left breast with the rope continuing down the back and tied to her right leg, which is raised up off the floor. Her right arm is further tied to a harness rope that she has around her waist. When her right arm moves to allow her right leg to touch the floor, the arm will pull on the harness and the rope threaded through her legs will rub against the sensitive areas of her genitalia.

Another predicament bondage scenario could have her harness rope connected to her neck collar, giving her just enough maneuverability to bend over in an uncomfortable position. If she were to straighten up, this would tug the harness against her genitals.

You can also perform predicament bondage with nipple clamps. For example, securing one end of the clover clamps to a male's nipple then securing the other end to his scrotum (or a woman's labia) will create an interesting situation. The slave would have to bend over slightly for this, since the chain that connects the clover clamps (nipple clamps) is only so long. As he's being flogged or whipped, he will instinctively jerk his body, even straighten up, depending on the severity of the impact of the instrument. This reaction will cause the clamps to tighten on his ultrasensitive body parts where the clamps were placed.

For men who are uncircumcised, you can place the clamps on their foreskin. Oh those delicious cries of pain they'll create! The Sadist will love it. You want to be sure to gather enough foreskin so as not to accidentally tear it. Remember the whole point of predicament bondage is to annoy or challenge and to set up a situation where the submissive creates their own discomfort and torment by moving.

As rope bondage can take hours, some Masters/Mistresses avoid using rope and opt for the quick leather cuffs or metal restraints, since for them, the fun begins once the submissive is tied up. Also, some Dominants don't want to be that intimate with the submissive/slave, and leather or metal cuffs work great. This isn't to say that these types of bondage can't be intimate, but that rope bondage creates a "different" sense of connection between the Dominant and the submissive.

The beauty of rope bondage doesn't end until sometime after the ropes are removed. The rope itself leaves behind marks and indentations on the body that will last for a few minutes or few hours depending on how long the rope was tied to the body. These rope grooves form their own erotic sensation for both the Dominant and the submissive.

At times some discoloration may occur, especially if the rope was used to bind the penis, breasts or other body parts in awkward positions. Personally, I don't find skin discoloration erotic, thus I avoid it. Plus there's also the safety factor of blood circulation to consider. When in doubt, play it safe is my motto.

For men, discoloration can also occur if he's been placed in genital bondage, and he becomes erect as his girth presses against the ropes, creating a pleasure/pain effect, causing the blood to pool into the tip of his penis, thus discoloring it. Not to worry, this discoloration will go away. If you maintain the arousal, the slave won't know whether to choose to be released from his bonds or beg the Dominant to let him climax within them—yet another form of dominance and surrender. A great book for CBT (Cock and Ball Torture) is *Family Jewels* by Hardy Haberman. Hardy provides wonderful ideas on ways to torment a man with his most prized possession.

With rope bondage, as with any other bondage or restraints, the Dominant must always make sure the slave has proper circulation. This can be checked by pressing your pinky beneath the ropes or beneath the restraint. If you can press your pinky comfortably beneath the restraints, you typically have enough leeway to prevent poor circulation. If not, the ropes need to be loosened to avoid permanent nerve damage. Another way to check for good circulation is touching the skin and fingers and feeling the coolness of the skin. Too cool and there may be circulation restriction.

You can also have the slave squeeze your hand while you notice if there's enough pressure when they do. If they're not in subspace, they should be able to squeeze normally; if they can't, this may be an indication of a circulation problem. These are basic tricks used by Dominants when checking circulation. I'm not a medical doctor, I am a clinical sexologist, and my rule is always, when in doubt, release the rope and rewrap it.

Of course conversing with the submissive is imperative to make sure the rope isn't over joints or isn't creating excessive discomfort. If discoloration begins, releasing the rope or repositioning the slave may be in order.

Before you begin any bondage session, you always want to take into consideration any physical and/or medical ailments the submissive may have, such as diabetes or circulatory problems that may affect their submission. This is definitely one of those times SSC/RACK should be observed.

The use of ties, scarves and nylon stockings in lieu of actual rope isn't recommended, as these items actually tend to restrict blood flow and become quickly entangled in knots. That beautiful $50 plus scarf or tie you love will most likely be ruined or have to be cut off after a night of play. One trick to getting a knot out that most people don't know is that if you roll the knot between your fingers or palms, it will actually loosen and allow you to unravel it easier. Remember patience is needed when playing with rope.

One item you always want to have handy when using rope is rope scissors. These are merely a few dollars, therefore you can purchase a few. Keep one in the toy bag, one in the dungeon, one in the car, etc.

Hoods

Hoods are a wonderful form of control and psychological play! Depending on the type of hood you purchase, you can control what the submissive/slave sees and hears, thus playing with sensory deprivation and taking the scene to a higher level of intensity. I've found that hoods allow the Master/Mistress to be more detached and sadistic with their slave than they would normally be, as they are not confronted with the face of their submissive and thus can objectify him/her more easily.

For Dominants who enjoy the aggressive nature of their slaves, they can designate the times the slave wears a hood as a free pass to allow their aggressive nature out to play without fear of repercussions. Then again being tormented because he/she was naughty is a reward in itself sometimes.

Of course, like the blindfolds, if the hood is used for sensory deprivation, it will affect the interactions of the slave as well as the Master/Mistress more quickly.

<u>Nipple Clamps</u>

Yes, nipple clamps hurt going on because they pinch, and prolonged or severe pressure will create cracking of the skin; however it is when the clamps are removed that the real pain begins, and the severity of the pain is in direct proportion to the length of time the clamps were left on. Thus a clamp left on the nipple for 5 or 10 minutes may be great when it's removed; however, one removed after 30 minutes produces major pain. As with other areas of the body needing circulation, you do not wish to go longer than 30 minutes not only because of the level of pain it will produce but also the possibility of nerve damage.

Imagine what it's like when your foot falls asleep and those needle-prick sensations rush up your leg. Now multiply that by 20, 30, even 50 percent. That rush of recirculation is what creates the pain and will bring tears and screams from the submissive. To minimize the pain, press your thumb or palm against the nipple to regulate and slow down the returning blood flow. Experienced submissives will actually beg you *not* to remove the nipple clamps after they've been left on for a while, because they know the agony of pain awaiting them.

Clover clamps are actually the best clamps to use, as they tighten when you pull on them, thus keeping a good grip wherever you place them. Nipple clamps can also be used on other areas of the body, such as the genitals, the male's scrotum, the underside of the arms, etc. There are larger and tighter clamps available for use with the scrotum. Purchasing clamps that incorporate a chain is best, as you can tug on the chain to torment the submissive further.

A great way to incorporate a mind fuck and have the slave torture themselves is to have them hold onto the chain attached to the clamps. Place the chain in their mouth, thus keeping it out of the way while flogging them. As they jerk their head, they'll pull the chain. Since the chain is only so long, lifting their head would automatically tug on the chain. And of course if they drop the chain, then that must mean they desire the Dominant to tug on it, doesn't it? Don't forget, it's the psychological effect that triggers subspace.

Nipple clamps can also be used on the tongue; however basic wooden clothespins work best for this purpose as they're bulkier and more uncomfortable. There really isn't a fear of the tongue swelling and causing breathing restrictions as long as only the front tip is pinched. Be warned, this activity will lead to drooling. Yet the Dominant can always punish the slave for drooling, even if he/she cannot avoid it. Besides, don't all naughty slaves deserve a good tongue lashing—or was that leashing?

Something to keep in mind: since men's nipples are smaller and thinner than women's, it's harder to keep them clamped. The clover clamps do a great job at securing them, since they tighten when pulled. The psychological effect on a man as focus is given to this part of his body, which is ultrasensitive and often overlooked, is astonishing.

Clothespins will also work well, as they have a larger surface and can grip more. Using clothespins around the scrotum or on the penis itself (especially for uncircumcised men) is beyond erotic. If you purchase the colored clothespins, you have a more decorative look as well. Care should be taken with the plastic clothespins, as these have a tighter grip than the wooden ones. Also, the smaller plastic clothespins can tear the skin if used in zippers (a line of clothespins attached to a rope that is then pulled to rip the clothespins off quickly one by one) or ripped off the body using a flogger or whip. Some Dominants will sandpaper the wooden clothespins to ensure a smooth surface to avoid splinters— especially given the delicate areas these clothespins will be placed on.

Vampire Gloves

These are gloves made of leather or soft fabric that have little spikes embedded in the material facing outward. The spikes are thin and less than a sixteenth of an inch long. Think a third of the size of a thumbtack but not as sharp. The Master/Mistress will run their gloved hand over the slave's body and occasionally press down or squeeze different body parts, such as breasts, penis or even spank the submissive's buttocks. This creates a wickedly sinful sensation.

Chastity belts

The ability to control the orgasm of a slave is a powerful aphrodisiac and highlights the power exchange, especially for men, as they are used to being sexual whenever they desire. Placing a slave in chastity leaves no doubt in their mind that their body is now the property of their Master/Mistress.

There are several types of chastity belts on the market for both men and women. Some are very simple and others are extremely elaborate. The entire purpose of the chastity belt is control.

Some chastity devices are specifically designed for the penis or vulva. Others incorporate both the genitals and the anus. Most devices are secured with an external lock. Some of the more elaborate chastity belts have an internal locking mechanism as opposed to an external one. There are several devices for men on the market made from a clear plastic material. Personally, I like metal cages. There is just something very medieval about them. Some male cages have bars, while others have the area completely encased in metal.

There are some chastity devices that incorporate plugs that are inserted into both the anus and vagina and are locked into place, adding the additional component of discomfort and arousal. As these are more invasive, the psychological aspect of control is more pronounced. Still other devices have vibrating dildos for their insertable pieces.

For men, there are chastity belts designed like cages, which make it difficult for him to become erect, and if he does, the bent or restricted position in which the penis is kept will increase the discomfort and pain he experiences. The fact that the Dominant controls the slave's ability to remove the device and end the discomfort further establishes the control and creates a pleasure/pain dynamic reinforcing the Dominant's control and creating a synergistic effect.

Most chastity devices have a built-in hole in them that allows the individual to relieve themselves without having to remove the device. The hole is enough to allow for urination but not penetration. If no urination hole is provided, the individual would have to ask for permission to relieve themselves, surrendering their control more profoundly to their Master/Mistress.

A metal device adds the essence of actual weight on the slave's hips, constantly reminding them of its presence. Though there are several devices for men that are clear plastic, cheaper and lighter to wear, they don't have the psychological impact of a metal device, something some Masters/Mistresses enjoy adding into the mix. Some devices are designed for prolonged use and individuals may be placed in them for a few hours to a few days or weeks. This extended duration reinforces the psychological component as well as the power exchange.

There are also lightweight plastic penal chastity belts, which can be quite handy for a slave who is traveling and wants to avoid metal detectors at the airport or who has metal detectors at work. Although be mindful of new TSA screening protocols. (I have to chuckle at this possibility.)

Don't forget that uncircumcised men left in prolonged chastity will have to clean daily beneath their foreskin. There are special swabs on the market for this. Daily cleaning can also become a ritualized event with their Dominant's presence or assistance, even if it is over the phone.

Chastity devices can cost anywhere from $75 to $2,000 or more depending on the design and their intricacy. Some are specially customized for the individual man or woman and are tailored to their body specifications.

Anal sex

Anal sex is one of those activities that most men and women consider taboo. Because of this, it is one of the areas and sexual activities that become most profound in a BDSM relationship, regardless of the gender dynamics.

Anal sex is also one of the activities most individuals get wrong and cause unnecessary pain. Here's a quick anatomy lesson. The anus is actually shaped like an S-curve and has two curves. Penetration that is done hard and fast and "straight in" will cause extreme pain and discomfort, as the penis or the strap-on will slam into the back wall of the anus. This incorrect penetration can actually lead to damage and rupture of the rectum and anal wall, leading to serious complications and in extreme cases death. A slow penetration is required. After penetration is achieved, a stronger, harder thrust can be employed.

Another fact most individuals overlook is that the anus does not produce its own lubrication. Artificial lubrication is essential to avoid micro-tears in the anus as well as minimize pain, though if the purpose of the penetration is to cause discomfort, to exert dominance, then no lubrication will effectively cause the pain desired.

Here's another must-know! Anything inserted into the anus that doesn't have a large round base or a handle/string to hold onto it or keep it outside the body will be absorbed and sucked into the rectum, necessitating a trip to the emergency room. The same is true for items such as alcohol or drugs introduced into the anus, as they are immediately absorbed into the bloodstream due to the thin lining of the anal walls.

Anal sex isn't just about penetration! There are many erotic and fun activities you can do, including teasing, anal rimming, finger and tongue penetration and, of course, the highly advanced and dangerous sexual activity of fisting.

I'd recommend that anyone interested in anal pleasure and play read a few books on the topic of anal sex to learn the basics. Two of my favorite books on this topic are *Anal Pleasure and Health* by Jack Morin and *The Ultimate Guide to Anal Sex for Women* by Tristan Taormino.

A new book that's come to my attention which addresses anal pleasure for couples in particular is *Arouse Her Anal Ecstasy* by David DeCitore. What I enjoy most about this book is that David focuses on the sensual aspect of pleasuring your partner providing various exercises and examples along the way.

Impact Play

Impact play can be performed with a variety of instruments. These instruments, or toys as they're called, can include floggers, whips, canes, paddles, etc., basically anything that is striking the body. To avoid actual injury to the submissive/slave, regardless of the instrument used, avoid striking joints and/or putting pressure on them. The kidney area as well as the eyes, face, and head should be avoided. Care should also be taken when striking the soles of the feet, as all the body's meridians (nerve endings) terminate there. Anything else is fair game!

It is best to strike on fleshy areas of the body, as the impact will be absorbed more readily. Skinny submissives tend to bruise easier and have less of a cushion to their skin during impact play. It is also easier to draw blood from impact play with skinny submissives.

When slapping the face, the Dominant should place one hand against the opposite check before striking. This will help minimize the whiplash effect on the neck and impact to the face, preventing damage to the neck or eyes. Yes, eye damage can actually occur from severe face slapping, as the retina may become detached from impact.

You want to avoid cracking a whip near the head area, as the whip is actually moving at speeds that break the sound barrier and it can damage the eardrum.

Though whips are great fun to use, they do take lots of practice. Many Masters/Mistresses have struck themselves with a whip now and again when they've caught a ricochet. Often the Dominant will have their free hand up to guard against the whip wrapping around them as it comes back when they're sliding it from side to side over the slave's body.

Bull whips aren't typically used (expect for show) as they will cut skin. Single tail whips are the norm. They provide a sting to the skin and though they can produce welts, cut the flesh and make the slave bleed, it takes much more force and repeated strikes for them to do so.

Candle/Wax Play
The trick to candle wax is the height from which you allow it to drip on the body. The closer to the body the wax is, the hotter it will be when it lands on the skin. The best candles to use are those 99 cent prayer candles you can purchase at most food stores. These candles are bigger and last longer, allowing for hours of fun. Another plus to these candles is the tall glass jars they come in make it easier for you to hold them without burning yourself and allows the wax to melt sufficiently to drip it slowly over the submissive's back, breasts, genitals or anywhere you desire.

Light a few jars at a time to have plenty of melted wax at your disposal to drip over your slave. If you purchase various colors you can also create art on their body.

Some Dominants enjoy melting a lot of wax, using a designated slow-cooker crook pot and brushing the wax over the submissive's body, then using a knife to carve symbols or words into it. The warmth of the wax will create its own unique sensations.

I once had a male Dominant convince me to allow him to brush the wax on my back. He swore it was the most orgasmic experience I'd ever have. Though I'm not submissive, I agreed to allow him to do so to see what it was like. Within five minutes of him starting to pour the wax over my back and brushing it on thick, I fell asleep. To me, it felt like being covered in warm clothing and so peaceful I promptly fell asleep. I opened my eyes once when he tried to "scare me" by telling me he'd use his knife to scrap the wax off my back. Since I trusted him, I merely fell back asleep. He did not appreciate my response. My failure to respond as he expected—as his submissives had in the past—frustrated him.

He insisted that if he poured the wax over my breasts I would experience the orgasmic sensation he was talking about. To appease him and my own curiosity, I allowed him to pour the wax over my breasts. Other than a slight heated sensation when he purposely dripped the wax closer to my skin, I again fell asleep, thinking of being covered in warm blankets and clothes just coming out of the dryer.

I share this with you to stress the importance of mindset and the psychological connection for the person receiving this or any other activity. To me it was warm and comforting, to others—submissives—it was erotic and orgasmic. To that Dominant male interacting with me, it was frustrating, as I didn't respond the way he expected and desired me to. Keep in mind that an individual with a Dominant personality will never respond with the same emotional connections as a submissive or a slave.

As candle wax is messy, you may wish to purchase a single bed sheet that you can discard afterward. Washing it would ruin anything that's in the wash with it and leave bits of wax behind to ruin other loads. To minimize ruining your bed or kitchen table, use an inexpensive shower curtain liner or plastic sheeting. (Again check Dom Depot; it's only a few dollars!) Place the liner underneath the bed sheet you plan to toss away or use the shower curtain liner by itself to catch all the drips and protect your bed, table, or carpet/floor.

For a person who's hairy, the wax will cling to their body hair, making it painful when removed. A trick to prevent the wax from clinging to the body hair is to use baby oil. Massage the baby oil over the body before dripping on the wax. Never use baby oil prior to fire play! This will actually burn the skin, as it will allow the fire to burn longer than desired on the body.

If you want to be erotically creative, use a knife or straight razor to help remove the wax from the body—even shave the submissive's genitals at the same time. Or you can use a thin comb and comb through the wax-matted hair on the chest or genitals for an added sadistic twist.

Another creative way to remove the wax from the body is to use a rubber flogger. However this will only work well if you dripped the wax on the body not brushed it on. This type of removal is messy, as the flecks of the wax will fly everywhere. This is better done outdoors or in a public dungeon, otherwise you'll be vacuuming bits of wax from the floor and furniture for weeks.

Fire Play
Fire play is an advanced skill and considered a form of edge play. Yes, it is very dangerous. It is definitely something an individual should learn to do with a mentor. It is performed in two different ways. One is by using a gauze stick dipped in alcohol and coating different areas of the body with it, then igniting the alcohol. The other way is by using gauze-covered metal sticks soaked in alcohol and already lit (on fire) and running them over the body.

The trick to fire play is in the timing! You don't want to leave the fire on the body more than a few seconds. One hand sets the fire, the other wipes it down and away. There is an erotic beauty in the way fire ignites on the body and how the blue flames rise, making the submissive arch and cry out as it heats their body. The Dominant isn't attempting to harm the submissive, so great care must be taken to prep the area and the submissive/slave to avoid accidents and injury.

As I mentioned earlier, never use baby oil or creams and lotions on the body before engaging in fire play. This will make the fire burn longer and can cause burns and blistering. It should go without saying that you want to avoid the face and hair areas.

There are a few technique/tricks that you can do that are fun and add to the eroticism of the act. One is when the Dominant brushes the alcohol on their palm, ignites it and then places the flamed palm upon the submissive's flesh. Another is what I like to call *fire spankings*: spanking the slave using the burning fire sticks.

Some individuals prefer their submissive/slave immobilized; others allow the slave/submissive the freedom to not be restrained, as accidents can happen, and if the submissive needs to move or "drop and roll" because of a spill or something, not being restrained allows them to do so. However, it also leaves the submissive/slave free to get up and run if they panic, which can cause its own risks.

Ensuring that the alcohol does not drip into any creases or body cavities where you can't immediately extinguish it is essential. Remember, the Dominant doesn't want to burn the submissive, merely provide them with a heightened sense of controlled fear. Another thing to consider is the fumes from the alcohol and flames, which will get to you after a while. Ventilation is a must! However, you don't want to have a fan blowing or the windows opened, because if there's suddenly a major breeze, it might take the fire places you'd prefer it didn't or blow out the flames before you're ready. Air-conditioned rooms are best.

Some submissives will quickly enter subspace because of the combination of fear, pain, and physical sensations they experience in their body created by this major endorphin rush. The Dominant will want to watch for enlarged pupils and slow responses or incoherent ones—all signs of subspace. Remember, a submissive will want to endure for their Master/Mistress, so they'll push themselves to take more even when their body isn't able to. It's the Dominant's responsibility to safeguard their slave and tame their own desires accordingly.

Hairy slaves should shave a few days before they engage in fire play. The smell of burning hair is a turn-off and definitely not erotic during a scene. Combining wax play and fire play may be interesting, especially if you're using the wax to remove the hair.

119

However, the skin will be extra-sensitive to fire play and the slave may not be able to endure as much.

For fire play you'll want to always have a fire extinguisher handy as well as a wet dish towel. The wet towel will serve as a way to cool down the body, and if any accidents occur or the fire is left on the skin too long and blisters develop, this will help. Have a can of sunburn spray handy as well. Spray this over the body after play, as it has a little bit of antiseptic and analgesic to help numb the skin and allow it to heal.

As I mentioned above, this is one of those activities you should be trained in before performing on your own. I do not recommend this activity for the beginner.

Fire play is all about the sensual connection and the eroticism. Care should be taken not to get drawn into the beauty of the flames!

Mummification

Mummification is a fun way to immobilize a submissive. The slave should be naked or wearing minimal clothing, as their body temperature will rise significantly—imagine being in a sauna. As the submissive/slave will have trouble standing and keeping their balance, you want to make sure there is a chair close by or somewhere soft they can lie back on or fall into.

If you are playing around water, be extra careful that the slave is able to breathe and remain in the shallow end of the pool. He/she will be completely vulnerable and helpless—even floating will be difficult for them.

Mummification can be performed with a few rolls of cling wrap and duct tape. Start out with putting the cling wrap loosely over the body areas you want. For example: around the shoulder and down to the wrist, trapping the arms against the sides of the body. You don't want to make it tight, as the plastic will automatically tighten as you circle the slave with the wrap. You can have the slave turn, however, I prefer the Dominant circle the slave since you don't want him/her to get dizzy. You can also just reach around them and layer the cling wrap around the body.

Here's another important element to add to your scene: Place a few cotton balls over the nipples when you start encasing the slave. The cotton balls create a buffer between their skin and the cling wrap. This will allow you to safely cut into that area once you're done wrapping them to expose their nipples so you can torment them as you please.

Once the cling wrap is in place, you can now layer on duct tape, which immobilizes them further. Again you don't want to put it on tight. The cling wrap will tighten on itself, and the duct tape on top of it will make it even tighter. You don't want the slave so uncomfortable there's a circulation problem or their breathing is restricted; this would require you to cut them out of it immediately. Also, you don't want to put duct tape directly on the skin, as it's difficult to remove and may tear the skin—especially in delicate areas. It goes without saying that you don't want to put duct tape directly on the hair or the face. Personally, I'd caution against placing it on the throat area, as you don't want to restrict respiration, especially if you also have the chest bound.

If you want to wrap the head with duct tape, use a hood in which the face is exposed or at the very least make sure the nose and mouth are exposed completely. Again, the Dominant must watch respiration and any restrictions to the same very carefully. (If the slave has asthma, have the inhaler handy.)

You can use arm-length pieces of duct tape to fortify the hold in specific areas as you desire. Using various colors of duct tape and cling wrap will allow you to be more playful. However the clear wrap will allow the Dominant to keep track of body color. Typically it will take approximately 20 to 40 minutes to completely mummify your submissive.

Once the slave is wrapped, the Dominant can play as he or she desires with their very own *live mummy!*

Engaging in sexual activities while the submissive is thusly bond is erotic and psychologically enticing: you would literally make the submissive nothing but a sex object, exposing only his/her genitals, anus, and breasts area.

When you're ready to end the scene, simply use a pair of scissors or a knife to cut the slave out of his/her bondage. With mummification, you want to slowly expose the skin to the air. It's essential to remember that the slave's body temperature will have risen significantly and exposing it too quickly can cause them to faint. Since they've been tied up, you want to make sure they don't tip over because they won't be able to break their fall. It's best to start releasing them by cutting away from the bottom, allowing the slave further access to their legs so they can sit down or lie down before you release them completely.

Be aware of subspace, which will affect their coordination and coherence. Another safety issue to keep in mind is that they will become dehydrated while wrapped, so have plenty of liquids (water) available for them to drink while mummified, especially if they're in it for an hour or more.

Never combine fire with mummification!

If you're doing any kind of breath play or waterboarding (an advance form of drowning), keep the slave at the shallow end of the pool. This is paramount for their safety.

I do not recommend waterboarding! This is an extremely dangerous activity especially without an assistant or when performed with a newbie who will most likely panic from the overload of emotional and psychological fears.

Mind Fucks

One of the most sadistic tools in the Dominant's arsenal is the mind fuck, or head trips as some call them. The beauty of the mind fuck is that by being evasive or creating a distortion in perception, a "double think" scenario were two truths coexist simultaneously, if you will, you confuse the mind and push the submissive over the edge without the need of any other instruments. The book, *The Forked Tongue* by Flagg has wonderful examples of how to create some exceptional mind fucks.

It's easier to give you a few examples of a mind fuck than to try and explain how to create them. Below I've provided a few simple examples of how they have been used in previous scenes.

The submissive was bound and blindfolded as he felt the knife against his flesh. At the last minute the Dominant turned her hand, dragging the sharp edge of the knife handle against the submissive's stomach. The submissive cried out, thinking he'd been gutted. This misconception was further reinforced when the Dominant stuck her fingers into a glass of water then ran them over the submissive's flesh in the same area she'd dragged the handle of the knife, using a wiping away motion and saying, "Damn, you're bleeding."

In another mind fuck, the submissive had been used hard and had some genital torture performed. When he'd put his underwear back on, the Dominant noticed that the submissive had dripped some ejaculate on the fabric but said nothing about it. A little while later the submissive stated, "My underwear feels wet." The Dominant promptly replied, "Oh, I didn't think I cut you that badly."

Though in each case there had been no real damage, the thought and the emotional connection led the submissive to feel fear and further psychological torment. Some submissives thrive on these types of psychological and fear-based interactions; others cannot tolerate them and break under the pressure, which is why mind fucks are at the top of the list of advanced edge play. Because of the psychological upheaval experienced, though it may be sadistically scrumptious for the Master/Mistress, it can be very emotionally draining on the submissive. You may find that the slave reaches subspace much faster than normal during a mind fuck. It's mentally and emotionally draining on the submissive, causing them to hit subspace quickly and once there unavailable to play further. Also, if the submissive panics or an old fear/psychological wound is triggered, the Dominant will have to walk them through it and/or end the interactions or redirect their scene. Then again, perhaps the purpose was to create "panic" and fear to help the slave overcome it and learn to desensitize that fear. The mind fuck has so many possibilities!

The major caution I can provide is to be careful with the issues and scenarios you pick to play with when engaged in mind fucks. Some themes can open up a door to emotional pain and the need for professional psychiatric treatment; and of course, a loving Dominant would never want that. You want to play rough with your toys but not break them!

***

It's essential to remember that much of what's done in BDSM affects the individuals not only physically but even more so psychologically, regardless of whether they're coming at it from a Dominant or submissive perspective. This psychological connection is why BDSM relationships are inherently much more intense and develop more quickly than vanilla connections even without physical/sexual contact. The need to belong, to serve another, to interact and feel powerful or connected is the driving force behind every Master/slave relationship.

A note of caution! Several of the ideas and interactions I've provided in this book and in this chapter in particular are considered edge play and are extremely dangerous to engage in. Please remember to educate yourself before engaging in them. Though I believe in RACK principles (Risk Aware Consensual Kink), I object to any edge play and even some basic play being performed without the Dominant, at the very least, educating themselves and learning about how to keep the slave safe.

BDSM is about a loving caring interaction with another human being, not a cavalier way of getting off on an erotic scene; the physical, mental health and well-being of both the Dominant and the submissive should always be the foundation of any interactions.

Chapter 8

Training a Slave
Protocols, Rituals & Corrective Measures

When a slave/submissive enters into a relationship, he/she is trained in the protocols and rituals of their Master/Mistress. Once these protocols and rituals are delineated, the submissive is required to adhere by them. If the slave does not, he/she is corrected, punished, and finally dismissed if all else failed to correct the situation and elicit the desired behavior. Let's break this down a little further for you to follow the concepts of each phase in training a slave.

<u>Protocols & Rituals</u>

The major difference between a vanilla relationship and a BDSM one is that there are specific guidelines that govern how an individual is to behave while in the relationship: what is acceptable, and what will not be tolerated, are hashed out and negotiated at the beginning and reinforced, expanded upon, and changed as time goes on. In a vanilla relationship it's assumed that each individual knows how to behave and knows what is expected of them, so that when they go against what their partner expected, fights ensue or the excuse "I didn't know" is used.

Protocols are a set of guidelines established by the Master/Mistress for the submissive/slave to follow to help them know how they are expected to behave and perform. These protocols may be elaborate or simple. The purpose of the protocol is to reinforce the submissive/slave's position in the Master/Mistress' life every time they perform the act. It also gives the submissive/slave a sense of belonging and accomplishment they may not otherwise have in their vanilla life. In case you're wondering, the submissive can also request a specific protocol or create a ritual that makes them feel comfortable or safe and share this with their Master/Mistress, having it incorporated into their actions when serving.

Below are a few examples of kneeling protocols for a slave to conduct when in the presence of his Master/Mistress:

Kneeling straight up to show respect with his hands at the small of his back and his eyes straight ahead or downcast is the common form of presentation and shows respect. The slave may be allowed to rest on his heels with his palms on his thighs awaiting the next command from his Master/Mistress.

Another position can find the slave kneeling supine, his body resting on the floor, arms outstretched as if bowing before a Queen and awaiting her next command.

Some submissive/slaves are allowed to stand instead of kneel, especially when in dungeons or at an outdoor event, or if the slave has knee problems. Under these circumstances, the submissive/slave may be required to stand in accordance with the prescribed protocol. This may be to stand at attention or parade rest as they do in the military while in the Dominant's presence. (Parade rest is where the submissive stands with their arms behind their back, their legs shoulder width apart, their head held high looking straight ahead.) You may consider this the slave's ready position,

Some Dominants institute eye-contact restrictions protocols: The slave is required to never look the Dominant in the eyes. This protocol reinforces the hierarchical mindset of BDSM. A submissive/slave would then be corrected or punished if he/she fails to adhere to it.

Some protocols require that a slave wear a certain type of uniform or wear nothing at all while serving. One Master/slave couple I know instituted a dress code in which the slave wears a plain white blouse with a long, dark-colored frock dress over it, along with flat-heeled shoes—a very conservative attire. The

Master also wears a type of Victorian suit that's very professional-looking and in keeping with his business responsibilities. If you met this couple, you would never think they were kinky. They look like your average wholesome Ma and Pa neighbors.

Don't forget what I said before about BDSM lifestylers being the people you see every day sitting next to you on the bus or at church or at work—or perhaps in the mirror.

The list of possible protocols is endless, and each Master/Mistress can tailor the protocols to what they require of their submissive/slave adding their own flair as desired.

On top of protocols are rituals. Rituals are established either separate from or in conjunction with particular protocols. For example one ritual may be that when the submissive/slave returns home from work, he or she is required to bathe, consciously and metaphorically washing away their vanilla persona, then kneel naked in a designated area.. During this time of quiet reflection, the slave reorients him/herself to the life they have chosen with their Master/Mistress and also release their outside worries and stressors. Once the designated time has passed or the slave feels they're ready, he/she would rise and go about their duties in the household and/or present themselves to their Master/Mistress as per the established protocols.

Another ritual can govern the way the slave/submissive offers themselves for use prior to engaging in BDSM activities with their Master/Mistress whether in private or in public.

Below is an example of a ritual a Dominant woman created for Her slave, which is used when they engage in public play.

The ritual begins with the slave preparing the area for them to use. The slave lays out a red lap blanket on the floor where she's designated they will conduct their scene. This serves to establish a boundary for onlookers not to cross. The slave then sets out the toys from her BDSM toy bag. He places a chair for her to sit on directly across from where he'll kneel to allow her to observe him for as long as she desires. By preparing the area, he shuts out everything from his mind. Once the scene is ready, he undresses completely and kneels on the blanket, closes his eyes, centering himself and focusing on being of service to his Mistress in any manner she desires of him. The slave may be embarrassed and feel vulnerable to be so exposed before others as he awaits his Master's dictates, yet he does so anyway as he knows it brings her pleasure to have him so exposed.

As the Dominant sits in the chair, she is able to observe her slave's diligence and attention to detail. In a way, she too is preparing herself for the scene to come.

The ritual continues when she joins him on the blanket. She strokes his hair and reassures him of her presence. Before she binds him, she raises his face so he may look into her eyes, brushes his lips with hers, nibbles his lower lip and tells him how pleased she was by his efforts. She then kisses his wrists before she places each wrist in leather cuffs, which she then connects to the ceiling beam overhead.

This is a sweet sensual ritual for this couple. Not all rituals have to be sensual, some are pragmatic, others are forceful. Everyone's protocols and rituals vary and are unique to them. You can put any twist you desire to them. The only thing the Dominant has to keep in mind is that He or She is responsible for reinforcing these protocols and rituals. If the Dominant isn't willing to put the effort into upholding them, they shouldn't be established as it'll create bad habits in the slave/submissive and make the submissive/slave wonder at the level of dominance they are actually receiving.

As I mentioned before, the submissive will often test their Master/Mistress and purposely mix up the protocols or rituals or perhaps not adhere to them to see if their "naughty" behavior will be corrected. This test isn't done out of childishness, disrespect, nor malicious intent but in an effort to reassure themselves that their Master/Mistress values them enough to care that they're doing a good job in following the established rules of the household and that the Dominant is willing to punish them when they're not.

Some slaves/submissives may demand a higher level of control, requiring their Dominants to impose "absolute measures and punishments." These slaves may leave a relationship if their more extreme needs are not met. Without these strict controls, the slave doesn't feel right about the relationship. There is nothing wrong with this. As we've discussed, every individual has their own needs and should find the best relationship for them—just as is done in the vanilla realm.

Before I move on to corrective measures, I want to talk a little about training a slave to accept pain and become orgasmic from it. Though the training is much like anything you wish the submissive/slave to learn, when training a slave to accept pain, you must slowly introduce it and connect it to their sexual release. You also make pain a reward they receive for being good, such as receiving a spanking or a flogging. The difference here is that you're constantly increasing the level of pain or emotional intensity associated with what would otherwise be a punishment. This emotional connection is what will eventually have the slave/submissive needing, even begging his Master/Mistress for more since he will have associated his pain with the pleasure of fulfilling his Master/Mistress' needs. In this way, you seduce the slave with his/her need for pain; and thus have also begun his pain training.

As for how you would punish a slave you are training to accept pain, you would withhold their ability to interact with you and share your time and essence.

Pain Training

A submissive/slave can be trained to enjoy pain, even learn to orgasm from it. The trick is to seduce them into it! This seduction is accomplished by using their own desires to achieve the Dominant's objective. For instance, the slave wants to please his Mistress/Master, therefore he/she will try to accept what the Master/Mistress desires and finds erotic.

The truth is that as the body starts experiencing pain and the adrenaline and endorphins as well as DHEA are released into the body, it can register the stimulus as either pleasure or pain. It is the individual who places a psychological and cultural significance to the stimulus, deeming it good or bad, pleasure or pain, which the mind and body will then accept accordingly. This is no different than the old belief of "no pain no gain" that athletes thrive on; or the military Rangers who use the fact that when they "feel pain," it's a reminder that they're still "alive."

In order to help the slave embrace the desire for pain or to be able to tolerate it better, the Dominant must link sexual and/or emotional gratification to it, having one sensation override the other and conditioning the slave to desire pain as a way to achieve pleasure. Employing Pavlov's salivating dog experiments (classical conditioning) and the principles behind behavior modification will help achieve this connection. I find that having the slave count through the pain allows him/her to be seduced into the idea that the pain will go way as soon as they reach a certain number. The counting also provides a sense of accomplishment, and the slave feels pride in him/herself that they were able to endure the pain for the duration of the count. This sense of pride is especially true for masochistic individuals as it serves to reinforce the pleasure/pain connection.

Of course, this feeling of accomplishment deserves a reward. The reward can be a kiss on the boo-boo or a sexual treat or another reward previously agreed upon of a sexual or affectionate nature. It can be anything the Dominant chooses to bestow on his/her slave for being so brave and enduring for them.

Corrective Measures

The natural progression of a slave/submissive when entering into a relationship is that he/she is trained, corrected, punished, and finally dismissed if all else fails. Here's how it works.

The submissive/slave is trained to do a specific task. If the submissive does not understand or does not follow through on what is requested or required, the submissive is corrected. If the correction provided does not remedy the situation, punishment is administered. If training, correction, or punishment doesn't correct the behavior, dismissal from service will result.

Below is an example of the natural progression to training a slave/submissive on performing a specific task.

The submissive is instructed that when he is told to present himself for inspection, he will stand with his arms behind his back, right palm over left, fingers flat not interlocked, shoulders pressed back, head held high, eyes straight, feet slightly apart

The submissive followed all the instructions; however, he erroneously placed the left palm over the right. His Master/Mistress will then correct the position, talking him through it once more. If he again errs, he is again corrected and made to perform the presentation several times until the Dominant is sure he has it correct. Tomorrow or a few days from now when he again is instructed to assume this position and fails to do so properly, the Dominant has several forms of corrective measures to use, whether that is to retrain the individual to reinforce the proper way to present himself or to use punishment.

Let's break down the corrective measures further, so that you may see what it looks like and how it leads to behavior modification. If you want to know how to institute change and the value of punishment, review a few therapeutic manuals on behavior modification as well as a few books on Dominant guidelines. For our purposes, we're going to get the "down and dirty basics" to help the Dominant elicit the behavior she/he desires from their submissive/slave.

It's imperative to remember that when dealing within the power exchange, there are only three choices when it comes to corrective measures. Understanding which comes first is essential in establishing the foundation of the relationship and ensuring it flourishes to its utmost potential. As with any other relationship, if you address the issues before they become problems and communicate effectively you can create a joyous union. If not, you'll create a nightmare you'll long to escape from, which will only serve to make you feel inadequate and frustrated. Nowhere is the old adage *you reap what you sow* more true than when in a BDSM relationship.

Corrective measures are not about making the person feel bad or humiliating the slave and should follow the pattern of training, correction, punishment and dismissal. Punishment should never be the Dominant's first choice. You want to build up to punishment not jump to the deep end.

Now, if the employee (submissive/slave) is provided with the adequate training necessary and is still not meeting the expectations, then correction is necessary. At this point, the supervisor will go over what is required and even have the employee recite the requirements to him/her to ensure the employee is correct and if necessary reword or clarify any confusion there may be.

As we continue with this example: if despite the training the employee was provided, he is still unable to follow through appropriately and still makes mistakes or his performance is not acceptable, then it's time for the employer to consider the following:

(a) Is further training appropriate?
(b) Does the ritual or protocol need to be changed?
(c) Should the employee be referred out for specialized training?
(d) Is punishment the correct next step or is dismissal warranted?

In a work situation, corrective measures could mean loss of pay or commission, even suspension. Specialized training can be instituted by assigning the employee to another boss or trainer or sending them to a specialized training course.

In a BDSM relationship, corrective measures could be physical, such as a spanking, flogging, even humiliation, or sending the submissive for training to another individual or organization (such as a Slave's Retreat like Catherine Gross and other individuals and various BDSM organizations provide). Again, this is no different than in the vanilla realm, where the employee would be sent to Human Resources for training or sent to an outside agency for management development.

If after a predetermined time the situation doesn't resolve itself, dismissal should be considered. A slave/submissive is advised that they will no longer interact with the Dominant and ties are severed. The submissive/slave will also have their collar removed.

Losing their collar is traumatic for a submissive/slave. They no longer belong to their Master/Mistress and any interactions in the future will be limited or nonexistent. This is as devastating as any breakup in a vanilla relationship, if not more so, because of the unique dynamics of the D/s relationship. Depending on the length of time the Master/slave were together, it can even be as traumatizing as a divorce.

Yes, I am purposely making the connections between the vanilla and the BDSM realms. It's important to realize that the two are intertwined and have the same emotional connections. People don't stop being emotional human beings merely because they enter into a BDSM relationship. These relationships aren't merely a compartmentalized part of someone's life, it is—in many instances—their core identity and who they are, despite not sharing it openly with everyone in their lives. Thus when entering into a BDSM relationship that isn't just for play or a one-night stand/one-kink stand, the emotional connections are strong.

The responsibility for lack of training and the dissolution of the relationship falls primarily on the Dominant's shoulders. It is the Dominant's fault for not guiding the submissive/slave where they needed to go; unless of course guidance was provided and the submissive chose not to follow it or constantly fought against it. At that point, dismissal is the most appropriate course of action.

As with any other relationship, if one party is constantly fighting or not giving their all, then that is not a relationship you want to stay in. And though women are often people fixers, always wanting to help improve the person they care for or love and make them better; in a Dominance and submission relationship, this can be very detrimental to the Dominant's mental health.

You can't force submission!

It is either freely given or it wasn't there to begin with. Besides, trying to force submission is like trying to force someone to love you—it'll never happen.

Often you'll read in a romance or hear in real life that the individual presented a "challenge," and they were taught to be a great submissive or slave. This does occur. However, there is a tremendous difference between someone being a challenge, and someone fighting the Dominant for their submission every step of the way. One you enjoy, the other you're tearing your hair out. And though everyone loves a challenge, no one enjoys beating their head against a brick wall repeatedly.

The closest way I know to describe this dynamic is this: imagine you like a man and you want to date him. He plays a little hard to get (a challenge) and you pursue him harder. This is good.

Now imagine he's gay. This is what it's like to fight someone for their submission. Mission impossible!

As for what types of punishment the Dominant would administer to a submissive/slave, this would depend on the offense and the nature of the Dominant. Every Dominant has their own manner of punishment, their own hard limits. For instances, a Master/Mistress who's service-oriented may provide the slave with a hated task or use humiliation. A Sadist or typical Dominant may use pain as punishment—a flogging or caning, etc.

Though a slave being inappropriate and disrespectful once or twice can be corrected through the use of punishment, if this is a constant thing, then he/she is not someone the Dominant would want to be in a relationship with as it'll be an uphill battle—again, the difference between a challenge and mission impossible. Realistically speaking, who wants to be in a relationship where their significant other disrespects them constantly? Staying in such a relationship shows lack of self-esteem on the part of the Dominant and a need to work on their own issues.

The same can be said of a Dominant who is constantly disrespectful to a submissive. Unless this constant disrespect is purposefully part of the dynamics of the relationship because both the submissive and Dominant get turned on by it, (remember we previously discussed how some people enjoy being humiliated), then this Dominant is actually pushing the bounds of the relationship and in some instances being abusive within it.

I previously mentioned the fact that many submissive women look for a Dominant man in the vanilla world only to find an abusive one instead. The same can be true for a submissive man. We cannot overlook the fact that some Dominants and submissives (men and women) may enter into the BDSM community with ulterior motives, disguising their malicious nature behind bratty behavior or a sadistic façade. Often members of the community can spot these individuals quickly, and word gets around about them. In the end, the BDSM community is like any other, you have your good and bad.

The ultimate punishment is dismissal. Once dismissed, the Master/Mistress may decide not to interact with the slave in any manner. The slave/submissive's collar will be removed and any financial connections will severed. If the slave was a member of the Dominant's household, he/she would be required to vacate the premises—much like what happens during the dissolution of a marriage.

So now that we've addressed the basic steps to incorporate into any slave-training program (training, correction, punishment, and dismissal), let's dabble into the heart of punishments and humiliation as a corrective measure and as actual play.

Chapter 9

Punishment & Humiliation Play

It may not surprise you to discover that humiliation play can also be used as punishment. However, you may be astonished at the emotional connection these two types of interactions have on the individual—both Dominant and submissive.

In this chapter I will provide you with various examples of humiliation play, which can be used as punishment, or to help motivate the slave/submissive, or to provide an emotional or sexual release. You'll also discover how humiliation play can be used as an aphrodisiac and how some individuals actually thrive on it.

As the connection between these two intensely emotional areas of Dominance and submission are at times indistinguishable, I want to start with punishment and lead into humiliation play. Whereas punishment is mostly for punitive reasons, like humiliation it can be used for erotic reasons as well. Let's start however with punishment from a punitive perspective.

<u>Punishment</u>

As I previously mentioned, the severity of the punishment should be in direct proportion to the offense committed. For example: the first time a slave/submissive is perceived to be rude his Master/Mistress can address the behavior with a verbal reprimand—thus following the progression of corrective measures we previously discussed. If this is the slave's second or third offense, he/she can receive a spanking. Punishment can also be administered if the slave did not follow through with a task or did not complete his task in the time allotted.

Punishment can take the form of a spanking, sending the slave to the corner for a "time out" (yes, like a disobedient child), or giving the slave an hour of practice getting into the position with which he struggles. The choice of corrective action and punishment is at the sole discretion of the Master/Mistress. Punishment can even be sending the submissive home and not engaging further with him/her that day, depriving the slave of the time they wished to share with the Dominant based on their own actions. And though yes, this temporary dismissal will also deprive the Dominant from sharing time with their submissive, the Master/Mistress never wants to reward bad behavior, otherwise they end up with a brat and no one enjoys a child throwing a tantrum even less so when the tantrum is being thrown by an adult slave/submissive.

A good guideline for the Dominant to follow is never to use a submissive/slave in pleasure on the same day he/she is punished!

Another important factor about correction and punishment is that it shows the submissive/slave that their Master/Mistress considers them valuable enough to correct their behavior. This correction and punishment helps strengthen the emotional bond between the two. It creates a measure of calm and peace within the slave: he/she realizes that someone will be there to call them on any inappropriate or dangerous behavior, making them feel appreciated and loved.

It is not uncommon for a submissive to at times purposely instigate punishment—most often he/she will do so on an unconscious level; however some slaves do so purposely and again this behavior should not be encouraged as it undermines the power exchange and is in fact very disrespectful on the part of the slave.

However should the Master/Mistress notice or feel that the submissive is purposely failing to complete the task, and this is a consistent pattern of passive-aggressive behavior, the Dominant may choose to dismiss the submissive altogether and discontinue this toxic relationship.

Keep in mind that punishment doesn't always have to be physical in nature. Some punishments can be psychological in nature, which at times can be more effective. Here's an example of a psychological punishment: tying a submissive up and then refusing to touch them, just leaving them tied for a period of time in an uncomfortable position. Don't forget to add the hourglass or egg timer to keep track of time. For an added twist, let them know beforehand that they'll have to remain in that position for two turns of the hourglass or two rings of the bell. Thus, they'll regret the fact that they thought they were almost done as the first turn of the hourglass was done only to remember they had one more to go.

Even worse yet is tying your slave up then using another submissive in front of them, showing your slave what he/she missed out on because of their own inappropriateness.

It's important to remember that just as Masters/Mistresses are territorial with their submissives and their property, slaves/submissives can be as well. They know a good Dominant is hard to find and will therefore not want to share them or risk losing their Master/Mistress to another submissive. As a result, this punishment is very effective. Plus, the Dominant can teach the slave that just because they must punish the slave by not allowing the slave to play, the Dominant doesn't need to suffer the same fate.

Male Dominants are more likely to engage in sexual activities with other submissives than female Dominants. This I believe is a cultural norm regardless of whether in the BDSM or vanilla lifestyles. Female Dominants can cuckold their male slaves, forcing them to watch their interactions with another man. It's imperative to keep in mind that because of the power exchange dynamics, a Master/Mistress can openly choose to engage in sexual activities with others, yet deny their submissive/slave the same liberties.

However playing with another slave regardless of gender can be a double-edged sword, as some submissives will require sexual monogamy from their Master/Mistress. Of course, once the Dominant gives their word on sexual monogamy, it cannot be broken (not even justifiably broken). It would destroy the trust the slave has in his/her Master/Mistress and the entire D/s relationship. Betrayal can go both ways and without trust, BDSM relationships are too dangerous.

Keep in mind there are many ways to be sexual within the BDSM community without actually having intercourse with another. Thus the couple's definition of sexual interactions will have to be explicitly defined. Therefore, if sexual monogamy was the agreed upon boundary in the relationship for both individuals, this does not prevent the Master/Mistress from using another slave to whip, spank, flog or tease in some other way. Gotta love those loopholes!

Punishing the submissive with something they hate or hate to do is also very effective. For example, if they hate to scrub toilets, making them scrub the toilet with their toothbrush is very effective punishment. If they hate peeling potatoes, buy 50 or even 100 pounds of potatoes and have the slave peel each one. Then have the slave cook every dish possible with those potatoes— mashed potatoes, potato salad, French fries, potato pancakes, potato soup, etc. The Dominant can then give the food away to friends or have them over to enjoy it, while the submissive is sent to his room or sent home and the meal is enjoyed without the slave's presence; thus, the slave isn't able to receive any praise for the food or feel good that the food was appreciated. Not only would the punishment be provided, it would also be reinforced by the slave's absence from the festivities as he is not yet deserving of their Master/Mistress' time.

Okay, I'm sure you're getting the picture here. I can continue with many more examples; however I believe you'll come up with some wonderfully devious ideas of your own.

Many of the examples I've provided in the humiliation play below can also be used as a form of punishment as well. If you want to be really creative you can emulate those old Hollywood Chinese Kung Fu Masters. For example: make the slave kneel on uncooked rice with a bucket of water in each hand. Or tie them down and spank them until their buttocks were black and blue. Some Dominants use a bamboo cane or similar instruments to punish until they draw blood.

Below are a few additional behaviors associated with reasons for punishment that you'll want to address and/or avoid with your submissive/slave. For the sake of simplicity and to avoid confusion, it's easier for me to address these issues and examples as if I'm mentoring another Dominant. If you're a submissive, feel free to share these with your Dominant.

A Dominant always wants to be careful of a slave or submissive who does things for the sake of punishment. This is evidence of an individual who's either a S.A.M. (smart-assed masochist—a major brat who lacks respect), or a player (someone who's there only to get off and will be a waste of your time).

A Mistress/Master who's not comfortable with administering punishment or doesn't enjoy it may want to pass a more masochistic slave/sub on to a friend and find one who's more to the Master/Mistress' temperament. It is not uncommon for some Masters/Mistresses to not participate in physical BDSM activities and desire solely service-oriented activities from a slave/submissive. However, if you want to keep this particular slave (the masochist), a great option would be to designate a friend or fellow Master/Mistress as the "Punisher." This would allow the masochistic slave to experience the punishment he/she needs, as you sit regally before him watching him be whipped by another at your command.

It's imperative not to "baby" the slave/sub during punishment but to reinforce the fact that "it's regrettable that his/her actions lead to this." If you want to throw in a little more into the punishment, you can have the slave hooded/blindfolded so he never sees the person that performed the punishment or have the person dispensing the punishment hooded adding to the mind fuck. Everyone is afraid of the hooded man—he has no mercy!

Another reason to punish a slave is if you notice the individual is leaving every decision up to the Master/Mistress. This can be a sign of complete surrender, which is wonderful; however, it can also be a sign of someone who wants to take *no responsibility* for their actions, and these slaves/submissives will become a source of frustration to the Master/Mistress. Though it's great to have a slave who surrenders completely, it's boring to have one that gives you no input and the feedback you need to push against to challenge you to be a better Dominant and/or give you that thrill of having really pushed your slave/sub into another level of physical/sexual surrender.

If the Dominant recognizes that his/her slaves are constantly getting into trouble or that negative behavior patterns are common in the relationship, these problems may be caused by the Dominant and not the submissive. The Dominant may not have appropriate or clearly established protocols or rituals for the submissive/slave to follow. In this case, the Dominant needs to do some internal work on themselves and perhaps undergo some training of his/her own.

A final reminder about punishment: Never reward a slave on the same day you punish them! The slave has to be reminded that their behavior was inappropriate and will not be tolerated.

Humiliation Play

Let's take a look at humiliation play. One of the primary focuses of humiliation play is behavior modification, as well as a catalyst to improvement and increased self-esteem. It may surprise you to discover that for some men and women it is a tremendous turn-on and aphrodisiac. On another note, humiliation also serves as a wonderfully creative source of punishment.

Men more so than women seem to thrive on humiliation, even connecting it with sexual desire to a level beyond the typical "talk dirty to me" phrases. Though there may be a psychological basis for this erotic connection, the actual possibilities vary and if you're interested, you can research it further. The simplest conclusion I can provide is the one provided to me by a submissive woman I know. She stated that as a woman she was used to being put down and humiliated in many different ways by various people throughout her life: the teachers who didn't think she was as smart as the boys and overlooked her efforts; men who catcalled as she walked down the street or thought they could paw her as she danced with them at a club, even lovers and family members who were inappropriate. Therefore, she did not want it as part of her D/s interactions. She went on to theorize that as men were used to being at the top of the food chain and didn't experience the humiliation women did or at the same level, they could more easily eroticize it.

Humiliation takes into account several different areas of a person's psyche and can vary in degrees of severity and purpose. To elaborate, humiliation play can include embarrassment, degradation, self-esteem issues, self-worth issues and more. It can be performed in private or public. It can be overt or subtle. It can be for behavior modification, correction of inappropriate behavior, for sexual stimulation, and yes, even for encouragement and motivation.

I can already see you shaking your head, telling me no one would use humiliation for motivation; yet haven't you goaded yourself into doing such things in the past. Haven't you once argued with yourself saying, "You're such a chicken if you don't..." merely to motivate yourself into taking that necessary but fearful step forward? Haven't you ever heard guys talking with each other, saying, "Man up, dammit? Or my favorite, "You throw like a girl!" when they want the boy to do better.

The simple truth is that humiliation is used by everyone to some degree. Parents use it with their children to get them to clean their rooms or behave, sprinkling the humiliation with a bit of guilt and shame as well. The parents aren't trying to be particularly hurtful or malicious, they're just trying to motivate and/or correct behavior. Here are a few examples:

Look at your room—do you live in a pigsty?

What will your friends say if they knew you wet the bed?

Stop crying. Take it like a man. Do you want them to think you're a baby?

Some teachers use humiliation in front of the whole classroom to push their students to do better or to curb unwanted behavior. I remember having to put gum on the tip of my nose in school and walk to the lunchroom with it struck there because I dared to chew gum in class during grade school. And what about the kids who couldn't read well but were forced to read out loud?

Before we judge these behaviors, let's not forget that the military uses humiliation to reinforce and create the soldiers it desires, taking humiliation to an art form that not only modifies behavior but establishes a new foundation and, ironically, builds self-esteem along with it. Spend some time with a drill sergeant or a traditional martial arts instructor and you'll be an expert in no time by merely observing their technique. Unlike the old drill sergeants who yelled and screamed at you, it's the quiet drill sergeants like the one in the movie *Biloxi Blues* with Matthew Broderick that you should fear the most. That's the true Sadist, the Master/Mistress who controls you by having you control yourself through fear and apprehension, even anticipation, of what He or She would do next. And like the military, your parents, and your teachers, the Dominant uses humiliation to create the slave/submissive they desire.

When looking at humiliation from a sexual perspective, it is important to remember that we all have our limits and our triggers. For example: calling someone a "whore" in public out of the blue may be embarrassing and lead to a confrontation. However, calling your slave "your whore" or telling them you "want to see how dirty your whore can be" allows them to overcome their inhibitions and embrace their slutty adventurous essence. It's amazing how having the slave call him/herself *your whore* opens that door. I dare say it'll give you a thrill as well.

With men, I find that using their fear of their penis size inadequacies will attain one of two responses: either it'll make them more assertive and aggressive, wanting to prove to you what else they have to offer, or it'll make them meek and submissive, opening the door for you to attain further service from them as they desire to make up for their shortcomings in other ways. Even using their sexual experience against them of their explored or unexplored desires for same-sex interactions will foster control for the Dominant.

Though you may see some of these examples, as well as some of the ones below as degrading or immoral, consider for a moment that it is a power exchange between two individuals who do so with a conscious desire to be open to each other in this way. One being vulnerable and the other the aggressor—the catalyst for whatever emotional or sexual needs the activity fulfills for the two parties—and most important of all, it's consensual!

Again, I'll remind you that this behavior is not pathological in any way. It is merely a form of power exchange and perhaps sexual gratification, as well as emotional release and healing that can be experienced in a D/s relationship. Sometimes, working through a humiliation scene allows the individual a way of releasing the pent-up negative emotions they stored in their psyche, in their body, which needed to be purged. In this case, the Dominant is working as a pseudo-therapist to help the individual work through the issue creating the break in the slave's armor that's needed.

It goes without saying that an intense humiliation scene requires tremendous aftercare, which an ethical Dominant would provide themselves or have another take care of. Also, it's often overlooked that not only is the submissive affected by an intensely emotional scene but the Dominant is as well—typically more so when the Master/Mistress had to push someone they care about or love to such an extreme and hear them beg and plea for them to stop or be pushed further still, in order for them to achieve the release necessary. Remember "no" and "stop" are not safewords; therefore the slave allowed the humiliation or punishment to continue.

Unfortunately, I cannot tell you how to know when this emotional release is reached. It is different in every slave, and it is something most experienced or natural Masters/Mistresses sense internally. It is like having faith in a way, as it's something you can't describe or quantify, you just know. It's an instinctive knowledge that can't be delineated yet can be learned with experience and dedication to the craft. It is knowing how far you can take a person before breaking them!

For those Dominants who don't have this natural instinct, whether because of lack of experience or because they're not in tune with the submissive, they can learn by watching the signs and body language of the submissive, and of course if he/she calls out their safeword letting you know they've hit their limit. However, most ethical Dominants will halt interactions before the submissive reaches critical mass—before they break. No one wants to break their slave! Good ones are too valuable and rare.

So what's it look like? What examples can I provide that will help you?

Below I have provided a few examples of humiliation techniques that can be used regardless of gender, as well as a few more specific examples that are gender-based. Feel free to modify these examples as you wish. Yes, you can incorporate and integrate physical and sexual components within your humiliation scene to reinforce ownership and/or push the slave further as you deem appropriate and/or as you desire. However, unlike with punishment scenes and interactions where a reward would be inappropriate as you are purposely "hurting" the submissive due to their own misbehavior; with humiliation play, you can reward them afterward with sex or physical stimulation—or merely loving care.

The trick to humiliation play is in your creativity and using it to mind-fuck the submissive/slave. And it can also be used as a form of punishment. The true essence of humiliation play and why it works so well at curbing behavior is pride. It is the ego—the slave's pride—that you want to push against. Tapping into their pride and ego will provide you with the results you desire to make the slave feel, whether it's for behavior modification, punishment, sexual abandonment, or merely torment. Don't forget, as I mentioned before, some submissives both male and female actually thrive on humiliation. It's that extra push they need to overcome whatever obstacles prevent them from embracing certain aspects of themselves fully. And let's not forget it can also be a sexual turn-on.

Examples of Humiliation Play Scenarios for Either Gender

Writing:

Making a submissive write 100 times, in pencil, "*I will obey my Master*," or "*Naughty boys/girls are punished and don't get to play,*" will actually work wonders at curbing unwanted behavior. Not only does it reinforce your control, it makes them have to consciously tell themselves whatever you have them write out. Requiring them to write it more than 100 times will actually lose the desired effect. You want to use what they already know, what's been ingrained into their psyche. We've all had this type of punishment used against us when we were little by parents or teachers. Having them use a pencil instead of a pen is also a psychological factor; it'll piss them off to be treated like a child. And let's face it, we all hated to feel like a baby. Also, having the submissive perform such a childish task is humiliating in itself; they're reminded for the length of its completion that their behavior was inappropriate and childish. I can almost guarantee they won't do whatever they did again. And if they do, then a higher level of humiliation/punishment should be instated.

The Dominant should make it a point to count each line written to make sure the quote or line given was actually written 100 times. It's not uncommon for a submissive to use this punishment/humiliation to test the Dominant's attention, so the Dominant never wants to neglect His/Her duty in this regard.

Corner Time:

As children we all hated to be sent to the corner for a time-out. Again, you're playing on the individual's pride and ego by treating them like a baby who can't behave properly and is sent to the corner to stare at the wall for however long You designate. To show that you're treating them as an adult whose actions are those of a child, you can have them kneel in the corner on uncooked rice with their hands behind their neck or at their lower back. You can even set a cooking timer to have it beep when their punishment is over. A timer that ticks off the seconds, like an egg timer—or better yet, an hourglass—adding a psychological component to the humiliation as it constantly reminds them of their misdeeds. We discussed this factor in the punishment section as well.

Another way to use corner time is to make a small circle on the wall about the size of a baseball using chalk. Now place a penny or small coin against the wall and have the slave/submissive lean forward and hold the coin against the wall with their nose. For submissives who can't kneel for long periods of time, you can have them perform this punishment standing up or sitting in a chair and leaning forward. The point is they must hold that coin against the wall the entire time using only their nose. If the coin drops for whatever reason, their time starts again. A good length of time is thirty minutes to one hour. Beyond that time, the psychological factor of the punishment can be lost. Of course, you can help motivate them to not drop the coin again by having them pull their pants and underwear down and lay across your knees for a quick spanking before they're returned to their task of holding the coin against the wall.

The Dominant should never interrupt a punishment or humiliation task that's given even if the submissive cries or tries to talk you out of it or begs to be let off or forgiven because they're sorry. Bad behavior should never go unpunished nor the punishment cut short. The Dominant can acknowledge the submissive's sincere regret then continue with corrective measures. He/She should stop the timer or turn the hourglass on its side for the duration of the encouragement so time doesn't run out while you're providing encouragement. Believe it or not this reinforces the commitment of the submissive to improve their behavior. Subconsciously, the submissive will remember that the Dominant/Master will hold true to what they say; something essential for the submissive to believe and trust, especially when they're interacting on other levels such as edge play or other physical interactions. Once the encouragement is over, the Dominant would begin the timer or reposition the hourglass and allow the task to be completed.

Much of what's done in BDSM affects an individual psychologically whether from a Dominant or submissive perspective, so reinforcing behaviors and/or connections should always take this into consideration.

Sleeping arrangements:

Sleeping arrangements are a major source of humiliation play. They can also be used to either punish or reward. A Dominant can have their submissive sleep at the foot of the bed or on the floor instead of in the bed beside them because of a transgression or as a way to reinforce that only a cherished submissive would be allowed to sleep with his Master/Mistress. Having the submissive/slave sleep at the foot of the bed or on the floor also reinforces the control and mastery of the Dominant. The difference between a vanilla woman demanding her husband sleep on the couch, kicking him out of his own bed, is that act is about anger and this is about dominance and the power exchange.

Another subtle from of humiliation and power exchange is having the slave wear nothing to bed while the Dominant wears a nightgown or pajama bottoms. This reinforces the power dynamics. If the submissive is shy, this requirement will push at their boundaries, helping them open up more and become more confident and sexually accepting.

For some women being naked will really push at their boundaries, as women aren't used to being naked anywhere but the bathroom or if they're alone in their own room and never for bed. A daring woman might sleep without underwear but rarely without a tee shirt or nightgown. For males who are used to being naked for bed, you can use the reverse and require them to wear pajama bottoms or a chastity belt to bed so they'll remember their penis is the property of their Master/Mistress, and it's exposed only at their command.

There are so many more examples I can provide, however I'm sure you are getting the gist of it. Warning: never use humiliation on any behavior you enjoy and want the slave to keep. You can tease them about their behavior, however if you use humiliation the slave may curb that behavior or erase it altogether from his/her repertoire.

Light Humiliation
Teasing & Embarrassing Moments

Before we get onto higher levels of humiliation play, it's important to realize that lower levels can elicit great rewards for both the slave and the Master/Mistress, as it'll encourage and allow the slave to go outside their comfort zone and do so in a safe manner, knowing they're accepted and cherished. It is using teasing and embarrassing comments that only the Dominant and submissive know about. For example the Dominant whispers in the submissive's ear something sexual or reminds them how "slutty" they were just hours before, which makes them blush in front of others. Even running a hand over the slave's rear briefly can be a little embarrassing and yet be totally acceptable in a vanilla setting.

Personally, I enjoy teasing a slave in public by word or deed in ways no one is the wiser. It allows him to feel wanted and pushes his boundaries a little bit further encouraging him to be "naughty." It also allows me to be naughty myself .as I share something with him that no one else knows about. Our secret!

Let me give you an example of what this looks like:

A few years ago, a friend took her slave with her on a book signing tour. She had him wear a collar around his neck that said WHORE in big silver letters. He wore it underneath his turtleneck sweater so no one saw or knew he wore it. Every now and then when he'd come to the booth to check on her or ask if she needed anything, soda, water, etc., she'd asked him to show her his collar. He'd blush and ask her not to make him do it. She'd merely tilt her head and wait patiently until he lowered his turtleneck to expose it. Once she gave him permission to cover the collar once more, he would pull her into his embrace. He didn't realize that she made sure no one else was privy to his actions or could see the collar. Though he was embarrassed, this game they played allowed him to become more confident in himself and accept his sexuality fully.

It's interesting that we often think men are comfortable with their sexuality when in actuality they can be just as uptight as women are—they just hide it better.

Public Humiliation

Public humiliation is very tricky. Some individuals will react poorly to it, and others will be too shocked at first to know how to react at all. Those who get a thrill from being humiliated will see it as a reward. It's all in how it's handled. I'll provide some examples and leave the rest to you.

One couple I know used humiliation play in public at a grocery store. The male Dominant yelled at his female slave when she dropped some items on the floor. He was pretty loud about it and degraded her a bit. Needless to say, some onlookers including the store manager came to the female slave's rescue, which the male Dominant used to his advantage by blaming her for upsetting the onlookers and making them think he was a bad man.

My major objection to this was that they engaged in nonconsensual play with others as the onlookers and store manager didn't know the full scope of what was going on. But when you look at it objectively, this is no different from a woman yelling at her husband in public calling him a jerk because he didn't arrive at the restaurant on time and they lost their reservations. Or because he got lost and didn't follow the directions *she* told him to follow. You'll also notice that it's more acceptable and easier to overlook when a woman insults a man than the other way around. The next time you witness this behavior I'm sure you'll wonder if this interaction is as vanilla as you once thought.

Another great example of using public humiliation from a sexual perspective (on either a male or female) happened to a slave I saw at a club who'd been restrained and was being flogged. The slave became very aroused as his Mistress stopped for a moment to run her hand over his back and buttocks. The slave began to gyrate his hips becoming more excited from the touch. The Mistress stepped back, stated loudly for all to hear; "What a whore you are, getting excited from being flogged." She then proceeded to flog him even harder, knowing that in his aroused state he could take more pain and that her words actually fueled his desire to suffer and endure more for her.

Sexual Inspection

On a sexual level, for either gender, an inspection can be one of the most humiliating activities they undergo. The slave can be required to strip before the Dominant and show their body in complete nudity. Requiring them to remove everything including their socks and shoes even their jewelry will add an additional psychologically component; it tells them that they can't use anything to adorn themselves and physically strips them of all possessions. They're standing before their Master/Mistress metaphorically and in actuality with nothing between "them." A very vulnerable experience!

The Master/Mistress can then take this sexual inspection one step further by circling the slave/submissive, commanding him to bend forward at the waist, as the Master/Mistress stands behind the slave. To add a deeper psychological/emotional component the slave can be ordered to spread their buttocks for the Master/Mistress to inspect their anus. Adding genital inspections and commenting on it heightens the effect. The Master/Mistress can then take this even further, commenting on the attributes or shortcomings of the slave's physique. The slave can also be required to strip in public and allow others to inspect him/her.

Gender Specific Humiliation

Though much of humiliation play is interchangeable between the genders, below are a few examples that are gender specific. I will provide you the information from a psychological perspective, which I hope will provide you with a better understanding of how the humiliation will affect the individual and how best to use it in your own interactions.

Humiliation play is one of those things you negotiate and develop together. When using humiliation play you need to be specific. Some men and women like to be embarrassed in public not majorly at times but little things here and there. Some like to be cursed at and called names even told they're worthless, so they can prove they're not or just feel comfortable in their own internalized concept of themselves

For Women
_When playing with women, using humiliation in the areas of makeup, weight, sexual appeal, sexual exploits, and sexual experiences will elicit very strong reactions. Below are a few examples. For the sake of simplicity, I will provide the examples as if you were doing them yourself.

Mess up a woman's makeup; drag your hand over her mouth and smear her lipstick then tell her she looks like a clown or worthless whore. If she cries, drag your hand over her face and mess up her eye makeup and mascara, even grab her by the hair and drag her before the mirror to show her how "ugly" she looks. That's very humiliating and degrading.

Finding fault with the clothing she wears will elicit a strong emotional response. For instance: how her dress/slacks are too tight or too loose, making her *look* like a whore or like a prude.

Sexual inadequacies are a major source of humiliation! The Dominant can attempt to degrade her by pointing out "how lousy she is at giving head" or how she just "lays there when he fucks her." And if you have her rationalize that she can't move because she's tied up, well doesn't that create another doorway for possibilities.

Humiliation can also be used to show the person's lack of participation as they're too shy to state what they like or how it feels when they're having sex providing their partner with feedback, even if it is just moaning or saying "it feels good." Or making her tell him how it feels to have him touch her, fuck her, put things inside her and get her to vocalize what she feels, then use it against her. For instance, telling her how wet and aroused she becomes when he's taking her, using her, even offering to give her to other men to use. The fact that her body is responding to the physical stimulus or sexual arousal he's perpetuating in her makes it difficult for her to deny the verbal accusations and/or connections he's making.

"I can feel how wet you are. You want me to let other men fuck you, don't you? Look how you tighten on my fingers just thinking about it."

The Dominant can drag his fingers coated with her desire over her face to mark her or have her smell and taste herself. (For men, making them taste their own essence, then telling them how disgusting they look doing that and/or that even a woman doesn't swallow can be very humiliating and degrading.)

You can get as explicit as you desire. The point is humiliation can be used for or against the individual. And don't forget that within a sexual context, using dirty words or being sexually explicit can become tainted with shame and guilt. These two conflicting emotions (desire and guilt) intensify the experience, as her body and mind battle against each other. This internal battle is what will propel her into subspace. It's this conflict that will create the short circuit, if you will, that will push them over the edge into bliss or sexual release, as their minds can't wrap around two conflicting realities.

For Men

For males use their *machismo* and their desire to be brave against them. You can train them to take more pain or more *whatever*, because it's for their Mistress/Master. Point out the fact that a "real man" can take 10 seconds of a particular pain and *he* can only take four. If he cries out after ten lashes, tell him another slave took twenty, or better yet, remind him that he took twenty last week but is now too much of a weakling to handle the same amount. With men, playing with pain becomes a matter of encouragement and seducing them into taking more—and when all else fails, use their pride against them!

There was a slave I knew who had a Prince Albert piercing on his penis. His Mistress would use clothespins to pinch the skin underneath, which is excruciatingly painful. Once she put the clothespin on, she'd tell him to count for her—1, 2, 3...counting slowly. She'd count with him. When he begged her to remove the clothespin because he couldn't take anymore, she would. She would brush against him softly and let him lean into her from his tied position, letting him catch his breath for a moment. She'd whisper that he could do better and take more, asking him if he wanted to please her; helping him—encouraging him—to take more—in essence seducing him into accepting the pain. He shored up his courage and they started again. When he insisted he couldn't go further, She would ask if he was a coward or tell him how disappointed she was that he wasn't as brave as she needed him to be or thought he was. This would motivate him into surrendering further—withstanding more. She got him to count slowly till 20 during their session. Afterward, she rewarded him for how brave he'd been and how proud she was of him for enduring so much for his Mistress.

Remember humiliation can be used just to tease the slave into pushing themselves further than what they thought they could endure and/or to elicit behavior modification, getting rid of the undesired behavior and attitudes.

It's imperative to realize that everyone has their own emotional connection to a particular activity, word, or act. It is those emotional connections that will deem the activity objectionable or acceptable. Where the activity is performed and whether it's in private or public, before a group of like-minded individuals or a vanilla crowd, or whether it's perceived to be done in anger or affection will affect the person's acceptance of the same. Because of these varying factors, the slave's emotional reaction will vary from being embarrassed, humiliated, degraded or erotic. How the play ends will also be a big factor in this play.

For instance, after all is said and done, will the slave be rewarded or punished? And if humiliation was used as punishment, then there will be the warning that if the behavior isn't corrected to the Master/Mistress' satisfaction, further action will be taken or the slave might just be dismissed altogether! Sometimes the fear of dismissal more so than the pain of a severe punishment or humiliation is more frightening, especially if their connection to the Dominant is strong and their standing in the household or their sense of belonging will be taken from them.

Remember, because of the emotional component, humiliation will draw forth strong reactions. Make sure to provide whatever aftercare is needed by the submissive/slave (and even the Dominant) to strengthen the bond between the couple.

***

There are so many more examples I can provide on various ways to incorporate humiliation into a relationship, whether for fun or for punishment; however, at this point I'm sure you get the gist of it. Remember, humiliation can be used just to tease the slave into pushing themselves further than what they thought they could endure and/or to elicit behavior modification, getting rid of undesired behavior and attitudes.

It's imperative to realize that everyone has their own emotional connection to a particular activity, word, or act. It is those emotional connections that will determine if the activity is objectionable or acceptable. Where the activity is performed and whether it's in private or public, before a group of like-minded individuals or a vanilla crowd, or whether it's perceived to be done in anger or affection will affect the person's acceptance of the act. Because of these varying factors, the slave's emotional reaction will vary from being embarrassed, humiliated, degraded or erotic. How the scene ends will also be a big factor in this play.

For instance, after all is said and done, will the slave be rewarded or punished? And if humiliation was used as punishment, then is there the warning that if the behavior isn't corrected to the Master/Mistress' satisfaction, further action will be taken or the slave might just be dismissed altogether! Sometimes the fear of dismissal— more so than the pain of a severe punishment or humiliation—is more frightening, especially if the connection to the Dominant is strong and their standing in the household or their sense of belonging may be taken from them.

Remember, because of its emotional component, humiliation will draw forth strong reactions. Be sure to incorporate whatever aftercare is needed by the submissive/slave (and even the Dominant) so that they will be will to endure future humiliation scenes, and more importantly, to strengthen the bond between you.

Chapter 10

BDSM Checklist

The thing to remember about the *BDSM Checklist* is that anything and everything can be added to it. From domestic activities (such as cooking and cleaning), to fetishes, to sexual activities, and service-oriented issues. The list is forever expanding as you and your relationship grows. Add what's most important to you. The things you don't desire should remain on the list, since it allows both parties to know what's not acceptable.

I recommend completing a new *BDSM Checklist* every six months to a year, as you will find dramatic changes in behavior and tolerance. Plus, it may give you ideas to consider and further your scenes. And of course, things the submissive/slave doesn't like are wonderful tools to use when punishing them. Plus more importantly, it will show you a little bit of the psychological makeup and the inner fortitude of a person, as well as their willingness to surrender and/or dominate.

Though in general a *BDSM Checklist* is often completed only by the slave/submissive to allow the Dominant to assess the slave's experience and willingness to explore, I believe that the Dominant should also complete their own list as it's important for the one who wields the whip to know their own limits.

Please note for the sake of simplicity, I will address you as the Dominant. I believe this will help you internalize the information provided and help you get a better perspective of the essence of the power exchange.

This list will provide you with wonderful ideas that you can incorporate into your scenes as well as help you understand the psychological makeup of the person you are interacting with. Noticing what activities are desirable or acceptable and when, will not only outline a particular erotic scene but will also provide you with ideas on coercion, affection, and consensual nonconsensual activities to conduct. Though remember what's acceptable in fantasy can get you tossed in jail in real-life or ostracized from some places and ruin your reputation.

Another thing to keep in mind is that what a person will do or explore will continuously change as they grow in experience, self-confidence and in the trust they share with another person. Thus what one person may be willing to do with "Tom," she/he would never do with "Harry."

The *BDSM Checklist* I've created also provides a place to note any medical issues, phobias, or physical limitations that will greatly affect how an individual—whether Dominant or submissive/slave—will be able to interact with others. For instance, if the slave has diabetes or circulatory problems, prolonged bondage is something you want to keep a close eye on to ensure there are no blood flow restrictions, something that can become life threatening or result in serious physical and medical consequences. You'd also want to know if the person takes insulin and when they last are to ensure they have the stamina for play as well as knowing what you should do if they become disoriented or faint. Also, if a person has claustrophobia, putting them in a cage or even tying them up and placing them in a closet may exacerbate this condition and make them violent or withdrawn, even cause a psychotic break. As you must realize, there's more to Dominating/Mastering another individual than merely knowing how to throw a whip.

My personal favorite question in the *BDSM Checklist* is the question of "Force." This is a major psychological and emotional window into the individual. Would the submissive/slave accept any activity he/she previously stated as a "Limit" if "Force" were involved? You might find that, given a choice, the individual would set a limit for themselves because of their cultural or societal norms; however, they would leave it up to their Master's discretion and feel comfortable with the activity when they "had no choice" and they would do it only to "please their Master."

Please note, when I refer to Force in this context, I am in no way suggesting the slave/submissive would desire an unknown assailant to truly force them into conducting or participating in any of these activities. This would be a crime! I am specifically referring to a trusted Master/Mistress whom the submissive/slave knows and trusts and therefore he/she would be willing to experience these more frightening activities from a seemingly nonconsensual standpoint.

Though all *BDSM Checklists* are different, below is the simplest way I know how to address the multitude of possibilities. Splitting the list into what the individual has done and what he/she would like to do is the first step. Once they've revealed this information, it's a matter of determining desires, limits, and whether they'd like to give up total control or be forced into doing so. Also, it's important to remember that modifications will play a major role into whether a person will accept an activity or not. Remember the example I previously gave about someone accepting a spanking with an opened hand but not with an instrument. And of course, those things they *hate* are always a sinfully wicked activity to use when you need to punish the slave/submissive or you desire to reinforce your ownership.

Don't forget force is a major turn-on! What a slave/submissive won't do willingly by choice they may do if required or forced to do so by their Master/Mistress. It's that little voice inside saying, "I had no choice in the matter, Master/Mistress, told me to…" This literally creates a free pass for the individual to be naughty— slutty—a whore! The use of force gives the slave/sub the ability to overcome their biases, fears, and societal norms and surrender completely. It's like saying, "The Devil made me do it." And we all know that makes being "bad" deliciously sweeter. Plus, it's a wonderful excuse, isn't it?

I've also broken down the *BDSM Checklist* into various types of activities to include not only what they've experienced and what they'd like to experience but also the various categories of activities which include: service, physical, sexual, edge play and force. Each activity can be further broken down into specifics;

however that would make this *BDSM Checklist* at least 10 to 20 pages long.

For example: service can be alone or with others present; for the Master or for someone designated by the Master; in uniform or naked. Sex can be further broken down by using protection such as condoms, with designated individuals, with strangers, as well as in public or private. Remember, that the individual may be willing to behave a certain way in private surrendering to the Master/Mistress, however in public the individual would buck at such interactions. Therefore I'll merely leave room for you to be more specific and to add anything else you'd like.

Below are a few examples to get you started in understanding the vast dynamics disclosed from a simple *BDSM Checklist* and the importance of information you can gain from it.

Example of a slave's Response to *BDSM Checklist*

Name: Zachary
BDSM Identity: slave
Date: December 10, 2010   **Initial List**: Yes
Limits: Monogamy –no same-sex contacts –condom sex only
Medical conditions: Right knee surgery September 5, 2010; can't kneel long periods. Asthma.
Emergency contacts/measures needed: Use Inhaler if I experience an asthma attack.
Phobias: terrified of dogs
Other issues: none

Rating:
1. Love it
2. Hate it
3. Want to try
4. It's okay—Take it/Leave it
5. Force (will accept if desired/forced by Master/Mistress)
6. Need Modifications (Explain)
7. Never again—Hard Limit

Have Experienced   **Want to Experience**

Activity	Giving	Receiving	Yes	No	Rate	Giving	Receiving	Yes	No	Rate
Massage	X	X	X		1	X	X	X		1
Spanking		X	X		2		X		X	2
Whips Single-tail				X	1		X	X		1
Kneeling	X		X		1	X		X		5/6
Anal Sex	X		X		1		X	X		1
Same Gender Sex				X	5				X	5
Serving Maid/butler	X		X		1	X		X		1
Cross-dressing				X	7				X	7

Explanations to items noted above needing modifications:

a. Kneeling: i will kneel as Mistress/Master requires. i humbly ask that i be allowed to use a pillow as it is difficult to kneel for periods longer than one hour.

b. Inhale: my Inhaler is in my coat pocket. If I have difficulty breathing, giving me two puffs will alleviate the problem.

Let's take a look at Zachary's list. He identifies as a slave and it's understood that most of what he has experienced or will experience will be at the direction/discretion of his Master or Mistress. And though he stated no "same sex contact," this doesn't mean he wouldn't submit to a male Dominant or engage in sexual activities with the male Dominant since Zachary also indicated that he wanted to experience same sex activities if #5—*Forced*.

161

Zachary is service-oriented and loves giving massages and serving as butler. We can also assume that he is versed with the typical protocols of a slave, such as kneeling before his Master/Mistress. We immediately note what his limits as well as his phobias are, yet more importantly, that he has had surgery and he has asthma, which requires an inhaler. Therefore, the Dominant should ensure that before any interactions are engaged in, She/He knows where that inhaler is. It would also be good to have an extra one designated only for the play room or in the toy bag so that it's always available as this is a matter of life and death.

Knowing whether the slave/sub likes an activity or not will give you some insight into his level of surrender and whether he's an alpha slave or needs a strict hand. The fact that Zachary "loves" kneeling shows he enjoys showing his Master/Mistress respect and surrendering completely. However as you can see, he also stated he would allow his Master/Mistress to *Force* him to kneel. Though at first this may be confusing, it's really not when you take into consideration the fact that he's had surgery on his right knee and this can cause physical pain and even re-injury, depending on how far into his recovery he is. You'll also notice that he stated he would *Want to Experience* if he was #5—*Forced* and #6—*Modifications* were made. At the bottom of the checklist he stipulated what these modifications were. And if they're not there, the Dominant can include them as she/he reviews the checklist with Zachery and makes her/his own notations.

It should be noted that most slaves will want to please their Master/Mistress and will endure pain and discomfort for them. However it is the Master/Mistress' responsibility to keep the slave's well-being uppermost in mind and deny them this privilege until it will not cause them harm. An ethical Master/Mistress would forego a slave's kneeling until recovery was complete and provide him with an alternative to kneeling, such as standing with his head bowed and his hands behind his back. Or if kneeling causes only minor discomfort, the Master/Mistress may choose to force him to do so while providing a pillow for him on which to kneel and limiting the time spent kneeling, for example, 10 minutes instead of a half hour. Modifications can also be made to the kneeling position as he can be allowed to lean back and rest on his feet, which would take the strain off the knee as opposed to kneeling straight up, which puts all the pressure directly on the knees. And there are kneepads, which the slave can wear to minimize/eliminate the pressure on the knees. (These pads are the same worn by tile installers and rescue workers and can be purchased for $20 or so at most hardware stores or sporting goods stores.)

As we continue our review of Zachary based on his responses, you'll notice the *BDSM Checklist* shows that Zachary #2—**hates** spankings but would tolerate them at his Master/Mistress' choice. This is wonderful information to know, as you now have a tool to use when administering punishment or should you decide to torture/torment him in a scene just for your Sadistic pleasure. When you limit yourself to using the things he hates for punishment it reinforces your control as he would be unlikely to transgress in such a manner again any time in the near future. And the spanking (the activity he hates) becomes one which he'll associate with humiliation, further reinforcing the Dominant's control.

It's also important to know what activities he's experienced from the position of giving as opposed to receiving. Not only will this tell you whether or not his inclinations are those of a Dominant/Switch/slave/submissive but also what his role has been in the process. For instance, Zachary states he has experienced "giving" anal sex and loves it. However he has not experienced it himself as "receiving" was blank, but he would like to experience "receiving." An important discovery here is that he rated the activity of **Want to Experience** "receiving" as #1—*Love it.* This reveals that he has fantasized about receiving anal sex and "loves" the idea. Therefore, he would be receptive to the same. Now don't forget, just because he loved something in theory/fantasy doesn't mean he'll enjoy it after trying it. His next *BDSM Checklist* might reflect that he's experienced receiving anal sex and hated it and has even placed it on his limits list.

If we continue along the anal sex path, connecting what we already know about Zachary with what else is possible, you find that he has never experienced same gender sex but is willing to try the same if #5—*Forced.* This opens the door to many erotically enticing scenes and ways to mentally torment him or excite him with the idea.

163

More importantly, the fact that he would accept it if *forced* states two things:

(1) he would surrender all to his Master/Mistress; and

(2) he wants to be able to bypass the guilt associated with the activity.

And though you notice in the "Limits" section that he stated "no same sex contacts," he also stated he'd want to experience it if forced. This is something to discuss beforehand. It is an excellent example of *consensual non-consensuality.*

As we continue with our review, you'll notice one of his #7—**Hard Limits** is Crossdressing. This hard limit is something to be honored. You can tease him about it, but never cross the line or you'll destroy trust and of course it stops being consensual and crosses into abuse.

As you review the *BDSM Checklist* for the slave/submissive, you'll want to notice if the individual is leaving every decision up to the Master/Mistress. This can be a sign of complete surrender, which can be wonderful; however, it can also be a sign of someone who wants to take no responsibility for their actions and these slaves/submissives will become a source of frustration to the Master/Mistress. Though it's great to have a slave who surrenders completely, it's boring to have one that gives you no input and thus doesn't give you the feedback you need to "push against" to challenge you to be a better Dominant and to give you that thrill of having really pushed your slave/submissive into another level of physical/sexual surrender.

Let's take a look at one more example; this time from the Dominant's perspective. Notice what the Dominant likes and how she/he identifies as a way to not only build erotic scenes but also expand their personality. You'll notice if a Dominant enjoys more of the edge play scenarios and whether they've actually experienced them. Sometimes loving these activities and experiencing them from a Master/Mistress perspective is not about fear of trying, but fear of releasing the "*Beast*" within. It's also important to realize that these interactions will be shared with some and not with others. As I previously discussed, some women struggle with their desire for control and sadism as society has taught them women should never behave that way.

<u>Example of a Master/Mistress Response to the *BDSM Checklist*</u>

Name: Jessica
BDSM Identity: Mistress/Sadist
Date: March 25, 2014
Initial List: 3-years' experience

Limits: <u>Men</u>
Medical conditions: <u>None</u>
Emergency contacts/measures needed:
<u>Josh (212) 555-xxxx friend, fellow Dominant</u>
Phobias: <u>Heights</u>
Other issues: <u>none</u>

Rating:
1. Love it

2. Hate it

3. Want to try

4. It's okay—Take it/Leave it

5. Force (will accept if desired/forced by Master/Mistress)

6. Need Modifications (Explain)

7. Never again—Hard Limit

	Have Experienced					Want to Experience				
Activity	Giving	Receiving	Yes	No	Rate	Giving	Receiving	Yes	No	Rate
Spanking	X				2					2
Caning	X				1	X				1
Kneeling		X			1		X			1
Anal Sex	X						X			3
Same Gender Sex					7					7
Whips Single-tail	X				1	X				1
Knife Play	X				1	X				1
Fire Play	X	X			1/6	X				1/6
Breath Play	X				1	X				1
Orgasm Denial	X	X			1	X	X			1
Threesome Female, male, male					1					1/7

Explanations to items noted above needing modifications:

a. Fire Play: Josh should be present as am still learning

b. Hard Limit: Male Dom can have his female slave present in the room during the

Threesome however she can observe only. (Note: When playing with Josh, we can

have his slave tied to the wall and forced to watch. Josh enjoys torturing her that way.)

As you review Mistress Jessica's *BDSM Checklist* you'll notice that she's been in the scene for three years at minimum. You see she has no medical conditions and her only phobia is heights. You notice that she identified as a Dominant and a Sadist. She provided a contact number for a friend and specified him as a kink friendly individual and fellow Dominant so if there are any problems, the person calling can be open and honest about the situation.

As you beginning to go down her *BDSM Checklist,* you may be surprised to see that she indicated spanking was #2—*Hates it* but caning was #1—*Love it.* Though this may seem a contradiction since the activities of spanking and caning are very similar and both incorporate the buttocks, it's important to remember that the emotional connection to each is different and thus it's not unusual to dislike one activity and love a similar one.

As her self-identity in the lifestyle goes, she enjoys the more sadistic sides of BDSM and has experience with it. She did note under fire play that she #1—*Love it* and had #6—*Modification* necessary for it. As you review her explanation, she states she'd like her Dominant friend Josh to be present as she's still learning.

Giving anal sex is something she #1—*Love it;* however, she has not personally experienced it herself but would like to try it. It shouldn't surprise you that woman enjoy *giving* anal sex since this is one of the most taboo-riddled activities there is in both the BDSM and vanilla realms. It is also a tremendous source of power and is often viewed as the ultimate surrender of a slave to his/her Master/Mistress. The fact that Mistress Jessica wants to experience it with her slave shows her trust in him and perhaps a desire to intensify their emotional connection.

She put #1—*Love it* for orgasm denial both *giving* and *receiving.* Now this will immediately identify her as sensually driven, as she would enjoy bringing her slave/submissive to a level of sexual need and frustration and keep him peaking before allowing him to reach his climax. The fact that she enjoys it herself merely helps to heighten the pleasure she derives in sexually tormenting her slave. This is also a wonderful characteristic to have in a Dominant as it shows her ability to be patient enough to drive them both to erotic heights.

Then again, you could always wonder just who is enforcing orgasm denial on her? Is she using her slave to heighten her desire, denying herself the ability to reach release or is she craving her slave's touch and denying herself the same until she pushes him so far that he shows her the darkness within himself, satisfying them both. And let's not forget that orgasm denial is a wonderful punishment to use on a slave.

Mistress Jessica has a hard limit on same-sex interactions between herself and another woman. However, she does not appear to have the same hard limit when it comes to her male slave interacting with another male as she enjoys threesomes. Keep in mind that her participation in a threesome does not indicate that she will permit her slave to interact sexually with another male, just that she enjoys interacting with two men simultaneously. You will also notice that she has made modifications in her hard limits to allow the presence of another woman who is bound and only able to observe but not participate in her interactions. Perhaps this is a sign of her not wanting another woman to touch her slave.

As you've noticed, there are vast quantities of data that you can attain from a simple *BDSM Checklist* not only from a physical and medical perspective but even more so from a psychological and emotional perspective as well.

Each list will vary depending on the identity of the person and whether they identify as Master/Mistress, Dominant, Switch, slave, submissive, Sadist or merely a kinkster. And of course, men and women will have their own particulars as well with their own emotional, cultural, religious and spiritual connections.

I recommend everyone complete this or a similar BDSM Checklist at least every six-months or at minimum once as year. It not only reminds you of what you've done and may want to improve upon, but it also shows you where you may be stuck and how you want to expand and explore, even if it's with a friend present while with your slave and/or Master/Mistress.

Feel free to make copies of the *BDSM Checklist* in this book for your personal use and/or purchase a set of the specially designed *BDSM Checklist* packets. (Also available online at www.bdsmthenakedtruth.com.)

Remember every activity, whether physical or sexual, can be further broken down into specifics such as spanking with your hand, spanking with a hair brush, spanking over-the-knee, etc. Get as specific as you want to as you create your *BDSM Checklist.* Feel free to add any activities you wish to perform that aren't on the list. You might even find that you save some activities to perform with specific individuals; and, as you grow in your comfort, you may explore more of these wonderfully erotic and sometimes intense and dangerous activities.

Feel free to use the *BDSM Checklist* I've created as a guide to help give you ideas on what deliciously wicked scenes you can come up with. Remember there's much more you can add to it and, of course, feel free to do so.

BDSM Checklist

Date: _____

Initial List/Subsequent: _____

Name: _____

BDSM Identity: _____

Limits: _____

_____

_____

Medical conditions: _____

_____

_____

_____

Emergency contacts/measures needed: _____

_____

_____

_____

Phobias: _____

_____

_____

Other issues: _____

_____

_____

_____

Rating:
1. Love it
2. Hate it
3. Want to try
4. It's okay—Take it/Leave it
5. Force (will accept if desired/forced by Master/Mistress)
6. Need Modifications (Explain)
7. Never again—Hard Limit

Activity	Have Experienced						Want to Experience				
	Giving	Receiving	Yes	No	Rate		Giving	Receiving	Yes	No	Rate
Services											
Collars											
Gags											
Kneeling											
Blindfolds											
Restricted eye contract											
Protocols											
Rituals											
Butler/Maid											
Sissy Maid											
Foot worship											
Feminization											

	Have Experienced					Want to Experience				
Activity	Giving	Receiving	Yes	No	Rate	Giving	Receiving	Yes	No	Rate
Sexual Activities										
Sex (without condom)										
Vaginal										
Fellatio										
Cunnilingus										
Anal										
Rimming										
CBT (Cock & Ball Torment)										
Strap-on										
Same Gender										
Rape (consensual)										
Threesome (female, male, male)										
Threesome (female, female, male)										
Sex with strangers										
Gang bang										
Forced orgasm										

Have Experienced   Want to Experience

Activity	Giving	Receiving	Yes	No	Rate		Giving	Receiving	Yes	No	Rate
Roleplaying											
Religious Scenes											
Torture Scenes											
Vampire Scenes											
Predicament Bondage											
Age Play (consenting adults)											
Daddy/little girl											
Puppy Play											
Pony Play											
Prisoner/Warden											
Boss/secretary											

	Have Experienced						Want to Experience				
Activity	Giving	Receiving	Yes	No	Rate		Giving	Receiving	Yes	No	Rate
Restraints (any kind)											
Metal Handcuffs											
Rope Bondage											
Flogging											
Whips Single Tail											
Whips--other											
Nipple Clamps											
Spanking											
Spanking (over-the-knee)											
Spanking (Implement)											
Caning											
Chastity Training/Control											
Medical Scenes											
Needle Play											
Videotaping											
Mummification											

Have Experienced   **Want to Experience**

Activity	Giving	Receiving	Yes	No	Rate		Giving	Receiving	Yes	No	Rate
Humiliation Public											
Humiliation Private											
Suspension											
Sensory Deprivation											
Predicament Bondage											
Orgasm Denial											
Crossdressing											
Physical/ Restraints											
Bondage											
Hogtied											
Straight Jacket											
Chains											
Movement restriction											
Cages											

Activity	Have Experienced					Want to Experience				
	Giving	Receiving	Yes	No	Rate	Giving	Receiving	Yes	No	Rate
Edge Play										
Breath Restriction										
Fire play										
Inverted Suspension										
Abduction scenes										
Blood Play										
Branding										
Electrical Shock										
Urethral Sounds										
Fisting										
Knife Play										

	Have Experienced					Want to Experience				
Activity	Giving	Receiving	Yes	No	Rate	Giving	Receiving	Yes	No	Rate
Mind Fucks										
Interrogations										
Fear Play										
Phobia Play										
Hypnosis										
Force										
Same Gender Sex										
Waterboarding/ Drowning										
Anything else										

Explanations to items noted above needing modifications:

_____
_____
_____
_____
_____
_____
_____
_____

Other issues which could affect interactions:
(medical/physical/emotional/past history)

_____
_____
_____
_____
_____
_____
_____
_____

Possible interactions with others/strangers:

_____
_____
_____
_____
_____
_____
_____

Deliciously wicked thoughts to try:

_____

_____

_____

_____

_____

_____

Anything else/Comments:

_____

_____

_____

_____

_____

_____

Notes/Thoughts:

Chapter 11

Resources

Below I've listed a few resources for you to explore not only from the perspective of reading materials which will aid in your research and understanding of this uniquely complex lifestyle but also a few mass market videos that will help you see how the concepts of BDSM are portrayed in a semi-positive light.

I have also provided you with the names of some of great organizations within the BDSM community that yield a lot of valuable information both in education and legal issues. Though I don't have the room to list every organization in the country, I have referenced some of the ones on the East Coast I know personally and have worked with at times. For organizations in your area, review the Internet. You should be able to discover some in your local vicinity. Sometimes the closest one to you may be an hour or two away. It's worth taking the time to seek them out.

If you're interested in learning about BDSM and participating in some fun and informative workshops combined with a safe and discreet place to learn and/or play, indulging your voyeuristic tendencies as you build up your courage, or merely want to allow your curiosity a little taste of a few activities, research the Internet for local groups in your area and their upcoming events.

If you're adventurous and would like to attend a four-day or week-long function, below are a few major events (on the East

Coast) that you can easily find on the Internet which will provide you with hours/days of fun: BDSM Writers Con (New York City), Floating World (New Jersey), Dark Odyssey (Washington, DC), TESFest (New York City/New Jersey), and Shibari Con (Chicago).

Texas has several well-known organizations that hold yearly events in Dallas, Austin, and Houston. There's even a "Male Slave Hunt" planned by one organization I know of. I'm not sure if it's true that they grow everything bigger in Texas but I think I'll have to participate in that "Male Slave Hunt" just to be sure. And wouldn't that be a wonderful story to tell and read!

Most of these events have "Open Play Areas" (dungeons) that are equipped with various equipment for your enjoyment. There are always cleaning stations in the dungeon, which hold accessories such as antibacterial wipes and pads to use on tables, even condoms and lube where sexual activities are permissible. The equipment in most of these events includes a variety of crosses, spanking benches, metal cages, A-frames where you can tie up your slave/submissive, designated rope play areas, including fire play areas, and needle play stations, etc. You can usually play in the public dungeon after the workshops or during open dungeon hours. There's always something or someone to watch, and if you have questions or want to try something new or merely practice throwing a whip or try your hand at bondage, there's typically someone who's willing to help.

Most of the events have begun to offer additional areas specifically designated for a particular gender or sexual orientation. For example: the event may have a Men's Only Play Room, a Lesbian Only or a Transgender Only play room, along with the open play areas where anyone can play. These areas are not segregated because of any disparagement to the group. They are actually provided at the request of these groups, who have some members who feel more comfortable playing among individuals with the same sexual orientation and gender identity as themselves.

These events are reasonably priced and closed off to the public once registration capacity is met. Therefore you don't need to fear that someone will walk in from the street and gawk at you. And if you do bump into a neighbor or coworker at the event, rest assured that they're there for the same reasons you are. So either say hello or stay at the other end of the dungeon.

There are of course dozens of events each year throughout the United States held in hotels or on various campgrounds. There's even one event held in the desert. Below are just a few of my favorites.

Organizations

BDSM Writers Con

BDSM Writers Con is the only conference specifically geared toward writers and readers of dominance and submission. We bring together award winning authors in the genre as well as BDSM expert to provide you with valuable information and Live Demos on Dominance and submission with over thirty workshops to choose from. We also host a private BDSM Club night to allow you experience the lifestyle first hand and play with the equipment in a safe comfortable environment. There are various Mix & Mingle events for authors and readers to get together, plus much more. BDSM Writers Con is founded and hosted by America's BDSM Expert, Dr. Charley Ferrer. To learn more visit: www.BDSMwriterscon.com

Institute of Pleasure

I established the *Institute of Pleasure* in 2005 as an extension of the work I was already conducting in private practice with Sex Therapy, Relationship Coaching/Mentoring and education on sexual health. The *Institute of Pleasure* took my practice to the next level, including Sex Research, Medical Physician and Mental Health practitioner education, as well as women's and couple's retreats. I also collaborated with other sexologists around the country and in Latin America. I developed *the Dominance and submission Therapy/Mentorship* model and began helping couples who wished to embrace this area of their lives. In 2010, we opened a new avenue for sex education by providing consultations and workshops specifically tailored to writers who needed assistance in technical/psychological aspects of BDSM to help them complete their novels. I look at this as a way to help further educate the public through your books—your accurate knowledge—as you share aspects of this unique and controversial lifestyle.

The *Institute of Pleasure* also provides education on sexual health to the general public; conducts therapeutic services in person, over the Internet or via phone; and conducts research on ancient cultures' sexual behavior/practices as well as those practices and behaviors of our generation. You will find various workshops offered dealing with BDSM, as well as other relationship and self-empowerment workshops. We will be conducting Webinars (virtual seminars held online) as many of our patients and participants live outside the New York City area. Visit www.bdsmforwriters.com or www.instituteofpleasure.org for more information.

Doctor Charley.com
I provide Mentorships and private telephone consultations to help individuals embrace their Dominant or submissive personalities and discover the truths as well as dispel the misconceptions. I am a Kink-Friendly Sex Therapist. I do not judge and believe we all have a right to our sexual desires and beliefs. I provide Mentorships for individuals and couples in BDSM structure, polyamory, establishing power exchange structures and more. I provide six months and one year Mentorships. I also provide general and Sex Therapy therapeutic services. Please feel free to contact me for a FREE 15-minute consultation. Or visit my website and contact me to get started. Learn more at: www.DoctorCharley.com

Carter Johnson Leather Library
The Carter Johnson Leather Library is the only kinky library on wheels with over 10,000 pieces of Leather and fetish memorabilia from the 1700s to the present. This unique library is a treasure trove of BDSM information, rare books on sexuality, articles, and even posters and commemorative pins. It began as the private collection of Viola Johnson who so elegantly stated in 2010 that she had gone from the "library's keeper and creator" to its "custodian," keeping the memory of the Leather Community's origins intact for generations to come.

Amazingly, Viola rescued many books from local landfills and from those who wanted to destroy the books, magazines and pamphlets due to their own prejudices and fears. The library's motto is: "Never again Landfill. Never again Flames," and highlights the plight of the BDSM community as it struggles against the prejudices and social restrictions against it. As a nonprofit 501(c)(3) organization, all donations to the Carter Johnson Leather Library are tax-deductible. And of course, they accept anonymous donations.

Best of all, you can invite/hire this traveling library for your next event. Imagine the wealth of information you'll receive and provide to your participants. Plus, Mama Vi as Viola Johnson is known, will treat you with such loving care and respect as you sit with her and listen to how she found and rescued the books in her collection. I've no doubt you'll find incredible inspiration in this library. Visit www.leatherlibrary.org for more information.

Master/slave Development Center

This program is run by Sir Stephen and Sir Eric. These two individuals have a wealth of information related to the Master/slave union and BDSM Household development. Their courses are mostly focused on the development of the Master, helping Him/Her address their personal and emotional growth as well as enhance interpersonal skills that enable the Master or Mistress to attain the levels of skills necessary for a more cohesive union between themselves and their slave. I attended their *One-Day Seminar for Masters* and found it the most useful workshop and discussion I've had in years, as it helped me further understand and solidify my decision and identification within this unique lifestyle.

The skills taught by the Master/slave Development Center provide a doorway into understanding yourself and your emotional desire to *JUST BE,* putting you on the path to self-enlightenment as you establish your D/s relationship. To obtain further information about this valuable service, visit them at www.msdevelopmentcenter.com

National Coalition for Sexual Freedom (NCSF)

NCSF is a wonderful nonprofit organization dedicated to the political, legal, and social rights and advocacy of consenting adults who engage in alternative sexual relationships and lifestyles. They provide direct services, education, advocacy, and outreach to benefit the BDSM, Leather, Fetish, Swing, and Polyamory communities. NCSF holds a wealth of legal information concerning the rights of an individual's sexual expression and can provide legal statutes against consensual BDSM interactions in various states. A wonderful organization to support that is always in need of your financial donations. And as a 501(c) your donations are tax-deductible. For further information visit them at www.ncsfreedom.com.

Catherine Gross, PCC

Catherine is an amazing woman who approaches life with such *joie de vivre* that when I first met her, it made my heart smile. Her enthusiasm for helping others embrace their full potential in this lifestyle is inspiring. Through her popular workshops, A Slave's Retreat and Foundations in Mastery, Catherine helps men and women build the strong personal foundations that lead to creating healthy relationships. I recommend her as a resource to help you discover various aspects of the BDSM lifestyle and the personal struggles and ultimate self-acceptance of both the Master and slave. For further information visit her at www.foryourlifecoach.com.

The Eulenspeigel Society (TES):

The Eulenspeigel Society is a nonprofit 501(c)(3) organizations dedicated to the education and personal development of women and men in the Leather and BDSM communities. It is the oldest and largest BDSM support and education group in the US. TES offers a vast array of workshops and groups catering to Dominants and submissives, from both a male and female perspective. TES also has special-interest groups geared toward subsets of the community such as Dominant women/submissive men; Dominant men/submissive women; TNG—the next generation (for individuals 35 years and under); rope enthusiast; Switches; spanking enthusiasts, and many more. TES also holds a yearly event on 4th of July weekend at a local hotel in New Jersey that draws crowds from across the country. The amazing caliber of its presenters and the respectful community environment it has fostered is impressive. For further information visit www.tes.org.

ClubFEM International
ClubFEM International is an organization dedicated to the Dominant women/submissive men relationship. They provide education and activities for men and women throughout the U.S. and abroad. I am most familiar with the New York City area chapter and know there are chapters in almost every other city in the U.S.—if not, you can always contact the organization and start one.

The beauty of ClubFEM is its dedication to providing a safe environment where Dominant women and submissive men can enjoy a little play and socialize.

In 2010, ClubFEM in New York City hosted a Pony Romp in Central Park, which we were able to film for my TV Talk show *Pleasure*. Imagine human ponies ridden along the trails of this historical park, creating an opportunity for the community to join in and/or ask questions. Such a marvelous experience, I'll never forget. Look on the Internet and find the ClubFEM nearest you. For further information visit www.clubfem.com/international.

DomSub Friends
Dom/sub Friends is an organization geared toward the BDSM community. It provides parties and bi-weekly demonstrations throughout the year on various topics of interest to the D/s and sex positive communities in the New York City area, regardless of gender or sexual identity. As it holds its meetings at the oldest running dungeon in the country, participants can have a night out that's not only educational but erotically fun as well. The one thing I love most about this organization is its organizer, Viktor, who is always quick with a joke and a smile and makes everyone feel welcome. For further information visit www.domsubfriends.com

ShibariCon
ShibariCon is the world's premier international pansexual event that caters to lovers of rope bondage. This event is held

yearly in Chicago and provides amazing workshops. Its world-class instructors are among the best in the U.S. and abroad. The four-day event provides hours of hands-on practice and even has play space so you can put those hours of training to good use. Though I have not personally had the opportunity to attend a ShibariCon event, I have spoken to a handful of participants who have; however it is several of the individuals I've seen demonstrating their rope skills who have presented at the event who leave me craving some free time to be able to attend. For further information visit www.shibaricon.com.

Reading Material

The books I've mentioned below as well as those I've mentioned throughout the book are some of the best print resources on the market that I've personally read. By no means are they the only great ones available. I'm sure you'll find more on your own or if you have some you want to recommend, please feel free to email me or send me a copy. I'm always looking for more knowledge and information I can pass on to others.

Story of O by Pauline Reage

This is actually a very loving and romantic book featuring a Master/slave relationship. Its focus is on the male Dominant and submissive woman, and the dynamics of the relationships are beautifully and erotically portrayed. There have been several movies made based on the book; however, I've found they all lack the emotional connection that the book has. Then again, using your own imagination is so much more enticing.

Books by the Marquis de Sade

The Marquis de Sade wrote many books. One of the most popular was *Justine.* You might be interested to know that each edition of the book is somewhat different as are various other works by the Marquis. As the Marquis' books were rewritten and his life took turns which damaged him emotionally, his stories took on a harder edge. If you take into consideration his true love, his family circumstances, the period in which he lived (the French

Revolution) and the corruption of church and government as well as the reign of Napoleon, you may begin to see some of his writing as a result of his circumstances. However, as one of the "fathers" of Sadomasochism, his legacy will live on in infamy.

Sex Unlimited by Dr. Charley Ferrer
Sex Unlimited: The Ultimate Guide to Dating, Sex and Erotic Pleasure provides valuable information on how to enhance your sensual pleasure while dating or married. It provides various examples on Dominance and submission throughout the book and how to incorporate various sexual activities into your play. It takes sex from beginner to advance providing various ideas along the way. Sex Unlimited is a dating manual that provides not only relationship and self-awareness exercises but an entire chapter on BDSM, its dynamics, its potential, and several erotic activities to try with your partner.

Extreme Space: The Dominance and Submission Handbook by F.R.R. Mallory
Though this book is hard to find, it is a treasure trove of information into the phenomenon of subspace as well as Domspace and ways to deal with it. The information in this book is valuable and realistic and addresses such topics as adverse reactions and feral behavior in submissives, knowledge that actually saved my butt once. Therefore, I recommend it to every Dominant I know. A definite must-have!

The Forked Tongue by Flagg
If you want to know how to create those edge play and mind fuck scenarios we discussed, this book will leave you salivating and wondering why you didn't think of these possibilities sooner. *The Forked Tongue* will help you create amazing scenes that will have your submissive/slave begging for more.

SM 101 by Jay Wiseman
This is the entry book into the community. It has wonderful information and safety tips as well as various ways to play and keep yourself in SSC mode. Though it can get a little preachy on safety issues, it's a good read. This book was my intellectual or

should I say academic introduction into the BDMS community when I first discovered it in San Francisco while working on my Doctorate in Human Sexuality.

Different Loving: The World of Sexual Dominance and Submission by Gloria Brame
This is a huge book on the various aspects of BDSM. What I love most about this book is that it provides you with insight into the mind of the Dominant and the submissive by allowing you to read their words and thoughts. This book will provide you with amazing insight into the emotional connections individuals make in this unique community as you read their words and how various activities affected them.

The Sexually Dominant Woman: A Handbook for the Nervous Beginner by Lady Green
This book provides you with wonderful ideas to help your Dominant side get started. Don't worry that it's written for women, men can learn from it as well.

The Mistress Manual: The Good Girl's Guide to Female Dominance by Mistress Lorelei
Another wonderful book on how to embrace your Dominant side whether as a man or woman. Definitely worth reading twice and taking notes.

Family Jewels: A Guide to Male Genital Play and Torment by Hardy Haberman
A must read if you want to explore controlling a man in the psychological realms through his most prized possession—his cock! Hardy provides you with fantastic ideas on how to torment your lover in his "family jewels" and how to control his every move. This book is surprisingly in-depth and covers techniques as well as the psychological aspects related to the male psyche.

Movies and Videos
Videos are always a wonderful resource for you, especially if your time is limited and you don't have hours available to read. There are wonderful videos available for things like bondage or

mummification and a whole host of other D/s activities. BDSM videos featuring actual D/s scenes are an individual preference. Unfortunately, many of the ones on the market are just tacky, unrealistic, or specifically created for titillation. To find a good Dominant woman/submissive man's video, you'll have to hunt for it. However, don't feel guilty about indulging your voyeuristic needs—enjoy!

There are two videos I've noted below, which are the best BDSM themed videos on the mainstream market that depict Dominance and submission from a somewhat positive perspective, though they still have their shortcomings: *Secretary* and *Killing Me Softly*.

Secretary starring James Spader & Maggie Gyllenhaal

This amazing movie is not only touchingly romantic it's tastefully erotic as well. It provides you with a wonderful look at the struggles these two individuals experience in their attempt to discover who they are and become comfortable with their sexual desires. I especially enjoy watching the heartfelt performance by James Spader as he struggles with his need to dominate his secretary and yet conform to society's norms. Often this internal struggle a Master/Mistress undergoes to accept their dominant nature (especially for a woman) is not accurately portrayed. Yet it is one of the most important facets in the makeup of the individual and leads to the foundation of the relationships they'll share with another. This movie portrays this internal struggle brilliantly.

Killing Me Softly starring Heather Graham & Joseph Fiennes

This erotic portrayal of a couple embracing their BDSM connection has a few of the dynamics which you'll encounter when entering into such a relationship. The passion. The obsession. The need to connect with all aspects of the other individual's life. An amazing performance by Joseph Fiennes. And the breath play scene they engage in will make you hit the rewind button several times.

However, the downside to this film is that she starts questioning whether she's "sick" for wanting to submit to him, which is unfortunately a common theme in books and movies trying to portray the BDSM lifestyle.

Romance Novels

I tend to be very selective and loyal in my romance readings especially when I read a book for its BDSM storyline. I want to read a credible D/s story, not something that makes me argue with the storyline since I know the Dominant and/or submissive wouldn't really behave in such a manner in real life.

My time is valuable, I want **believable** fantasy. That said, if you want to see great BDSM stories in action not to mention phenomenal storytelling, I'd recommend my all-time favorite author Joey W. Hill, who has a marvelous way of showing and combining the psychological makeup and desires of both the Dominant and the submissive. Her Vampire series is a phenomenal and an erotically tasty treat with open and honest depictions of various BDSM interactions.

Jessica Lust, though not well-known, is an amazing BDSM writer. She tends to write on "forbidden" topics such as adult age play and more hardcore sadomasochistic interactions, which is why she isn't in the mainstream circles. However, you can find a few of her short stories around.

The most amazing aspect of Jessica's writing is her unique approach where she actually writes the story from a first person account giving you the feeling of peeking into someone's diary and sharing their thoughts. Jessica Lust also writes her stories based on input from friends and fans. If you want a scene or situation, she can create it; though in her style. She also writes private works on commission. You can contact her through at Jessica@JessicaLust.com

You'll also want to check out my latest website, BDSM WRITERS. It provides information on the latest BDSM books and writers as well as blog interviews, Live Chats, and their various contact information. You can even pick up a few of their books while you're there. www.BDSMwriters.com

And of course, if you join us for our yearly BDSM Writers Con, you'll be able to mix it up with your favorite BDSM authors and make new ones. BDSM Writers Con is the best way to appease your curiosity in a safe comfortable environment full of fun, entertainment, and most of all BDSM education for both authors and readers. www.BDSMwriterscon.com.

In Conclusion:

BDSM is like the ocean. It is forever moving, changing, evolving within you, and when you're not respectful of it, it'll drag you across its bottom and try to drown you. That said, it can be such fun playing in its waters, diving into its waves and exploring all the potential possibilities that you are as a person. You'll never find the same freedom in any other relationship that you discover in this one.

It is my sincere hope that as you explore this unique and erotic lifestyle, you do so with respect for yourself, your partner, and its participants. Keep in mind that to thousands of men and women, Dominance and submission is not merely an erotic way to get their sexual thrills, but it is a way of life. BDSM is sacred to them!

Allow yourself to learn and discover all you can. Join organizations, interview individuals in the lifestyle, go to workshops, even contact me at the *Institute of Pleasure* and join one of our upcoming workshops. I hope that *BDSM The Naked Truth* was able to provide you with a comprehensive insight into this unique, normal, and healthy lifestyle.

Live with passion,

Doctor Charley

About the Author

Dr. Charley Ferrer is a world renowned Clinical Sexologist and America's BDSM Expert.

She has over twenty years' experience teaching and exploring the world of Dominance and submission. The award-winning author of thirteen books on relationships, sexuality, and self-empowerment, Doctor Charley conducts workshops throughout the U.S., Latin America and the Far East, helping men and women to fully embrace their sensual and sexual birth right! Her charismatic approach to helping others has made her the "go-to" sex expert for various magazines, newspapers and radio shows. Dr. Charley Ferrer is the host and founder of BDSM Writers Con, the only conference dedicated to writers and readers of Dominance and submission. Doctor Charley loves to travel and explore the world. You can see pictures of her travels at her website www.DoctorCharley.com. She loves arts and crafts and creating stain glass panels.

She loves to hear from fans. Email her directly at doctorcharley@doctorcharley.com.

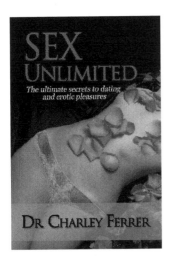

Sex Unlimited
The Ultimate Guide to Dating, Sex, and Erotic Pleasures

Whether you have just started dating or are searching for ways to breathe passion and fire into your relationship, Sex Unlimited is for you! Join world-renowned Sex Expert and Love Guru Dr. Charley Ferrer as she shares the ultimate secrets to dating and erotic pleasure. Doctor Charley provides candid examples and valuable information on how to become a world-class sensual lover, showing you how to break through the barriers that hold you back from exploring your full erotic potential. Discover the rich possibilities and various lovemaking styles in Sex Unlimited that will turn your fantasies into reality. This is not your grandmother s dating manual. No topic or secret is taboo! Experience the incredible journey to sensual self-actualization and embrace the sensual lover within. Doctor Charley's *Sex Unlimited* reveals the ultimate secrets to dating, sex and erotic pleasures!

Latina Kama Sutra

A sassy how-to sex manual that shows you how to flirt, be seductive, and enjoy erotic sensual nights. The first book on sexuality geared specifically for the Latino Community taking into consideration our unique culture, religion, and machismo. However it is perfect for any man or woman regardless of nationality or sexual orientation.

Whether you're shy or outgoing, male or female, Latino or any other nationality, The Latina Kama Sutra provides the secrets needed to reclaim your divine sensual and sexual nature to enable you to derive the ultimate satisfaction from every encounter. Regardless of whether you're flirting to get a seat on the bus or trying to seduce the lover of your dreams, you'll know exactly what to do to achieve your goal. Discover all those deliciously naughty ways to have fun with your partner whether it's dressing up, role-playing, or…well…you'll just have to use your imagination. There's even a special bonus section for men on how to overcome certain delicate difficulties.

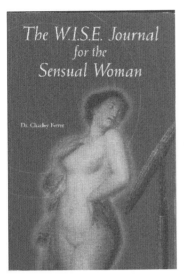

The W.I.S.E. Journal for the Sensual Woman

Dr. Charley Ferrer, world-renowned Clinical Sexologist, guides you along the page of sexual self-discovery as you learn what barriers prevent you from experiencing your full orgasmic potential. Discover the causes of sexual dysfunctions, how to work through physical disabilities, and whether it's possible to be sensual and engage in safe-sex. Through self-exploration questions, you will begin to reclaim your orgasmic potential and derive unparalleled sexual satisfaction. If you've ever experienced dissatisfaction in your sex life or suffered from low sexual desire, this is the book for you. Unleash your sensuality and claim your divine sexuality!

BDSM for Writers

Let America's BDSM Expert, Dr. Charley Ferrer, lead you through the intricate world of Dominance and submission.

Learn to understand the psychology of this uniquely erotic lifestyle, so that you can develop stronger and more realistic characters, plots and scenes.

Here is all the information you need on the basics of BDSM, including descriptions of the various personality traits of lifestyle practitioners. Discover the truths behind a Master/slave relationship and the intricacies of the power exchange to help you blend reality and fantasy credibly for your characters and erotic BDSM scenes.

Explore more advanced topics such as how to train a slave and the benefits and pitfalls of reward and punishment. There's even a full chapter on the various ways to use punishment and humiliation on a male or female submissive. Doctor Charley provides real-life experience and lifestyle tidbits along the way. Any author seeking to bring authenticity to their writing about BDSM will find Doctor Charley a knowledgeable world-class instructor and exceptional mentor.

28919176R00114

Made in the USA
Charleston, SC
26 April 2014